PROFESSIONALLY DRIVEN

EMPOWER EVERY EDUCATOR TO REDEFINE PD

PROFESSIONALLY DRIVEN

EMPOWER EVERY EDUCATOR TO REDEFINE PD

JAROD BORMANN

New Berlin, Wisconsin

Professionally Driven: Empower EVERY Educator to Redefine PD

The Bretzmann Group, LLC
jbretzmann@bretzmanngroup.com
www.bretzmanngroup.com

Publisher: Jason Bretzmann
Copy Editor: Cory Peppler
Cover Designer: Kelly M. Kurtz
Project Coordinator: Kenny Bosch

First Edition
ISBN: 0692950419
ISBN-13: 978-0692950418
Printed in the United States of America

ACKNOWLEDGEMENTS

My high school sweetheart and wife, Jackie. Your unwavering support on this journey, as well as ours together through life, is something I am thankful for and do not take for granted.

My three kids - Braxton, Tenley, and Jace - who keep me busy and help me see the learning process through a child's eyes.

The Oelwein professional development planning team of Steve Westerberg, Jill Kelly, Lori Decker, Kristi Druvenga, Dianne Loughren, and Diane Sperfslage, for asking the questions necessary to help shape the original vision for this model.

Officemate Bev Berns, for being a great thinking partner and encouragement on this journey and for sharing the title.

The Keystone AEA for their example of how adults could and should learn, as well as their continued support of the Professionally Driven journey.

The Professionally Driven educators who have taught me, who I've had the honor of working with, and who I continue to meet every day through my PLN. You have and continue to show me what it means to constantly out-teach my best teaching.

Jarod Bormann

CONTENTS

Foreword by Dave Burgess 1

My Journey 3
    Traditional PD vs. Personalized PD

Growth Mindset and Professional Development................15
    The Process of Moving Mindsets
    Choosing Fight
    Only a Growth Mindset Can Empower a Growth Mindset
    Turning Caterpillars into Butterflies
    Strengths Born from Weaknesses
    Getting Gritty
    From Point A to Point B
    The Purpose of PD
    Identifying the Weak Spot
    Lower-Levels to Upper-Levels
    Jarod's Story
    Finding and Filtering the Weak Spot
    Questions to Consider

Professionally Driven Educator: Jen Servais 41

Intrinsic Motivation and Professional Development.......... 45
    Training vs. Learning
    Rewarding Compliance vs. Recognizing Learning
    The Hero's Journey & Professional Development
    From A Hero's Journey to a Professionally Driven Journey
    Drive the Whole Journey
    Questions to Consider

Professionally Driven Educator: Mary Beth Steggall 67

Sustainable Autonomy and Professional Development.......71
    Sustainability Killers
    What is Sustainable?
    Think Like a Caveman
    Traditions = Sustainability
    Questions to Consider

Professionally Driven Educator: Liz Hill 97

The Professionally Driven Model **99**
The Process of the Model
Make the Process Personal
Recognizing the Learning Process
Structuring Time for the Process
Getting Started
Tight vs. Loose Implementation of the Model
Questions to Consider

The Coaching Role **123**
Coaching Guide Questions
Conversations Matter Most
The Checklists
Supporting the Process
Keeping the Learning Organized
Questions to Consider

Professionally Driven Educator: Jill Kelly **141**

Climb the Mountain **145**
Reaching My Summit
Continuing the Journey

About the Author **155**

FOREWORD

I have never apologized, backed away from, or held any reservations about declaring teaching to be the mightiest profession in the world. It is the profession from which all others flow. Education is at the very center—the root—of all progress. We are literally life-changers. In *Teach Like a PIRATE* I wrote, "We are superheroes wearing the Clark Kent disguise of teacher" and my opinion has only been strengthened and validated by what I have seen as I travel around the educational world.

If we accept, as I do, that teachers are the single biggest determinant of student success in our school systems, then it stands to reason that building their capacity to teach more powerfully, influentially, and effectively is of the utmost importance. Time, money, and energy are finite resources in districts all across the world. Therefore, we need to ask where we can best apply these resources to have the most impact. The answer is simple: professional development. Powerful PD is the Archimedes lever that can move any school or district to the highest levels of success.

The problem is that one-size-fits-all professional development continues to be the norm, even in an educational climate that has moved further and further towards embracing differentiated instruction and personalized learning for students in its classrooms. What about us? If these latest educational innovations have been proven to dramatically increase student learning, then doesn't it make sense that they may increase the learning of *educators* as well? After all, the best teachers I know are the ones that still see themselves as works in progress and are continually looking for new ways to improve. They are learners. They are students of their profession and calling.

This book is a model your school can follow to transform professional development and bring a much-needed variety to the way it is delivered. The Professionally Driven model will explain both *why* changes are needed and *how* to start your school out on its own unique path. When your school begins this journey, educators will move mountains to sustain it and intensify it because they will be in charge of their own adventure.

If beginning this journey seems outside of your comfort zone, all the better! That is where all progress is found. I tell teachers all the time that safe lessons are a recipe for mediocrity. The same is true for our professional development. I want to be energized by PD. I want to leave more on fire about my profession. I want to leave feeling more excited about getting back in my classroom and to feel more equipped to do powerful work. Educational leaders have to walk the talk. Don't talk to me about innovation, risk-taking, collaboration, connectedness, and creativity if the professional development you provide models none of this.

Do you want teachers to build innovative, collaborative, and empowering lessons that reach all students in your classrooms? Then start by implementing a Professionally Driven model in your school or district, and get ready for your teachers to be exponentially more driven to add to the life-changing experiences they create for your students.

Dave Burgess *is the New York Times Best-Selling author of* Teach Like A PIRATE: Increase Student Engagement, Boost Your Creativity, and Transform Your Life as an Educator *and co-author of* P is for PIRATE: Inspirational ABC's for Educators. *He is a highly sought-after professional development speaker well-known for his creative, entertaining, and outrageously energetic style. His workshops, seminars, and keynotes not only motivate and inspire teachers, but also help them to develop practical ways to become more creative and engaging in the classroom. Dave empowers teachers to embrace the mighty purpose of being an educator and sparks them to design classes that are life-changing experiences for students. Dave specializes in teaching hard-to-reach, hard-to-motivate students with techniques that incorporate showmanship and creativity.*

Twitter: @burgessdave
Website: DaveBurgess.com

CHAPTER 1
MY JOURNEY

It was my first year out of the classroom. I had only been teaching for eight years, but I was ready to put my new master's degree in instructional technology to work at Keystone, a state-funded area education agency that serves eight counties in the rolling hills of NE Iowa. After using technology to teach in my own MS/HS English classroom, I was ready and motivated to help other teachers use technology to get students thinking and learning at a higher level.

I still had my reservations with this new role, however. I loved teaching, and while this new endeavor was exciting, the idea of leaving my students left my stomach churning every night for months, both before and after starting my new role. I never paid attention to how much I made financially as a teacher, because I simply didn't care. I loved it that much. When I was offered this new position, I told my wife, "If I don't get the same sense of satisfaction, I'm going back to the classroom."

"Jarod?" I recognized the voice over the phone.

"Yes?" I replied.

"This is Rhonda. Say, I wanted to give a heads up about a school district that may be giving you call asking for some help this summer."

"O...K?"

"They're going 1:1 in the 6-12, I believe, and they couldn't fill their Tech Coordinator position for this coming year. They got a hold of me asking what kind of assistance we could provide for the year, because you know going 1:1 is a pretty large undertaking. So I told them that we have a new guy, you, that may not be quite as busy since you're new, so I passed your name along, and you may be getting a call from Steve Westerberg, the superintendent. Hope you don't mind, but I thought this would be a good opportunity for you to get your feet wet here at Keystone. How's that sound?"

I took the position of Technology Integration Specialist at the Keystone Area Education Agency (AEA) in May 2014. In June, I received this call from Rhonda Sheeley. However, my contract didn't technically start until July, and I was OK with that. I was excited to start in my new position; I just didn't expect to get a phone call this early. I hadn't even gone through new employee orientation yet.

Rhonda was one of the Directors of Instructional Services at Keystone when I was hired but has since retired. When she speaks, you need to give your full attention. She talks fast, and you will most likely miss something if you don't keep up. Conversing with Rhonda is like watching Cirque du Soleil—while at times it may look a little chaotic with each performer representing a new tangent or idea, each one is working with the other in a much larger vision. Sometimes, Rhonda sees the vision, but all you see are the tangents and ideas tumbling in every direction. Our conversation continued over the phone, but like a detective taking a witness statement, what I gathered was:

- Oelwein (pronounced Ol-wine) is a 2A school district going 1:1 with MacBook Airs in grades 6-12.
- They couldn't fill the Technology Coordinator position due to unforeseen circumstances.
- They are looking for AEA support, weekly if possible.
- Steve Westerberg is the superintendent.
- They have instructional coaches for their elementary, middle school, and high school.

A day or two after my conversation with Rhonda, Superintendent Steve Westerberg gave me a call at home and confirmed much of what Rhonda told me, but one new detail made me realize the scope of the initiative: Oelwein has about 600 students in grades 6-12. Now, this may seem like a small population for some school districts, but in Northeast Iowa, this is a fairly hefty initiative, and I understood their concern for necessary support.

Oelwein was my first school in this new role as a technology integration specialist, and I looked forward to the opportunity. I assisted with their laptop rollout, helping students to set up their devices and login. The students seemed ready to use the laptops, but were the teachers? They'd had their own laptops for some time, but putting the same tools in the hands of students made some feel unsure.

Over the beginning weeks of the school year, I visited the district once or twice a week. This allowed me to develop initial relationships with a handful of people in the three different buildings and stay in communication with Mr. Westerberg. A few weeks later, I was asked to be a part of their Tech Committee to help plan professional development (PD) for their Tech PD days. These occurred once a month for two hours. I decided to stay relatively quiet at my first meeting, simply because I was just the extra support guy. I wanted to let the team plan based on their teachers' needs. After all, they knew their staff better than I did at that point.

They began to discuss topics that they felt were necessary in order for teachers to use the new laptops more effectively in the classrooms. The idea of including Google Drive and the many nuances that go along with that suite of apps was considered. Some of the Apple iLife apps were also added to the list. A few other ideas were mentioned, and I quickly saw the format resembling what I would call "a la carte" PD: a variety of topics where staff can choose which session to go to at that time. It's a format that I experienced in my previous district when we went 1:1 with iPads, and it's no different than the format of almost any tech conference. There's choice, but usually the choices are predetermined by someone else. (I'll address the problem with this later in the book, but I'm sure you are already catching on).

As the sessions were being hashed out by the three newly appointed instructional coaches, the two techie librarians, and myself, I noticed Mr. Westerberg was also staying relatively quiet with a look of discouraged thought. The more the discussion panned out to prioritizing what the teachers would need the most, the more his eyebrows fell. I vividly remember this look, because I had not seen it before in any of my other face-to-face conversations with him over the course of that prior summer. He always presented a friendly demeanor, one that always gave the time of day to listen.

I remember wanting to ask him if he had any input on the sessions, but he beat me to it. "I'm going to speak up here, and forgive me if I sound a little frustrated. I know we have teachers in this district that don't need ANY of those sessions up there. They're already doing all of those. What about them?"

Everyone kind of looked at each other to see if the other had an answer, but no one did. However, it was that single question that started for me a Big Bang effect. This BIG question created such an intense energy within me: *What about them?* I felt that question was the open door, the invitation to activate my own thinking when it comes to the process of PD. Mr. Westerberg was a superintendent for a number of years and involved in education for many before that. I could tell his frustration stemmed from the same conundrum that many schools faced with professional development: *How do we provide something that **all** educators **want** and **use**?* Mr. Westerberg continued to talk, but the energy and ideas within me could not be contained. This was the release, or the BANG part.

I quickly grabbed my paper copy of the agenda, flipped it over, and scrounged in my bag for something to write with while trying not to draw attention to myself. I began sketching something that resembled the four levels of what this Professionally Driven model is based upon: **Research**, **Integrate**, **Reflect**, and **Share**. Why these four? They feel...natural, instinctive. Something that doesn't require formal training. They feel like real recreational learning. You know, the kind you do for fun. Not only that, Mr. Westerberg's frustrations were also *my* frustrations when it came to PD. I simply asked myself, *If I could make PD what I truly wanted it to be, what would that look like?*

I then quickly pitched the idea of scrapping "a la carte" PD and suggested these four phases. There was a short silence at first, but questions regarding each phase quickly ensued:

"How will the teachers know what to research?"
"How do we make teachers feel like they're progressing?"
"How do we keep reluctant teachers from doing nothing but 'research' for the whole year?"
"Will we need to keep track of points of some kind?"
"Will we still do specific tech sessions?"
"Who leads the tech sessions?"
"How will teachers track their progress or learning?"

Mr. Westerberg's initial question opened the door for bigger thinking, followed by more questions, followed by more thinking. But it's still Mr. Westerberg's question that I always go back to when I think of PD: *What about **them**, the educators looking to go to that next level?* In this case, Mr. Westerberg was referring to the teachers, but I would argue that "them" should refer to **the adult learners**, or in this case, **the educators**. By using *educators* rather than *teachers*, we can also include administrators, paraeducators, and any other adult learners in your district. When you include all of these groups in the learning process, the question then turns into, *What about **us**?* For me, Mr. Westerberg's question also led to more thinking about how our current traditional forms of PD do a huge disservice to educators, and I was suddenly reminded of my first professional development ever, and I began to recognize the need for change.

TRADITIONAL PD VS. PERSONALIZED PD

It was my very first PD as a new educator in 2006. My first teaching job as a high school English teacher was at a very large school district, much larger than Oelwein. Well over 100 teachers shuffled into the library to see what that year's "yearly initiative" would be. Even though it was supposed to be teacher-learning time, no one seemed to be rushing to take their seat. Teachers were still conversing about which students were in their new classes or reminiscing about summer vacation with wishful remarks that it wouldn't have ended.

As the final teachers found spots to sit in the only open seats towards the front, the principal gave a little welcome and kicked off the afternoon of learning with an ice-breaker. The projector shot up a quote that read, "If I die, I hope it's during an in-service (professional development), because the transition to death would be so subtle." The teachers around me chuckled at the humor in that statement, some heartily while I sat awkwardly wondering what they found to be so funny. But it only took a moment for the chuckling to subside before we proceeded to experience exactly what that statement suggested. If we know that statement is funny because we find it to be true, then why do we continue to make professional development something that teachers don't value but instead joke about?

Traditional professional development has always been more of an inactive experience, one where the educator is a passive learner.

Here are seven reasons why traditional forms of professional development don't meet the real needs of educators as learners, and in contrast, how the Professionally Driven Model offers a more appealing alternative.

1. TOP-DOWN

In the traditional sense, professional development has usually been top-down. In most cases, an administrator or team of administrators designate what it is that teachers need to be learning. Working with schools, I often hear administrators say, "Teachers don't know what they don't know." My immediate reaction to this statement is, "Why do *you* know and teachers don't? How did *you* discover what it is that they should know?" In most cases, the administrator went to a training/conference where a paid expert disseminated knowledge of how education could and should change, after which the administrator went back to their school and disseminated that knowledge to the teachers. Or administrators will sometimes pay to bring the experts in to disseminate the knowledge face-to-face. This implies that real ideas with a positive impact on classroom instruction come only come from paid experts, passed down to teachers through some kind of bucket brigade that dumps the knowledge into the next pail.

We need to quit viewing the teacher as the fire that is last to receive the water and the expert as the original source of knowledge that we must pay to dip our buckets into. In contrast to traditional PD, the Professionally Driven model starts at the other end of the bucket brigade—with the teacher. It helps create the internal combustion that is necessary to ignite a passion for learning in the teacher and then lets it spread to other teachers. As William Butler Yeats has been famously quoted, "Education is not the filling of a pail, but the lighting of a fire." We have extinguished so many learning fires within teachers for so long that there isn't a single hot coal left to stoke a spark. Moveover, the idea that "teachers don't know what they don't know" implies that teachers cannot be trusted to discover for themselves what it is they don't know, or worse yet, that teachers are not even capable of it. This type of thinking is simply incorrect and toxic for a school's culture.

2. TARGETS LARGE GROUP

A common phrase in education is "spray and pray" or what some have labeled as the "shotgun effect." This refers to a single person standing in front of a large group and presenting information. The likelihood that everyone in the audience will retain all of the information is slim to none. One simply hopes that the information reaches the right people in order to have some kind of an effect. Ultimately, this leads to a very low percentage of learners actually retaining and using the information that is presented. Usually, it's only the teachers who needed the information and found it useful and applicable that end up integrating it into their classrooms. Therefore, we need to use a method of professional development that has this kind of effect for *all* educators.

I've sat in with PD planning teams that give out surveys to see what topics teachers want. When the results come in, inevitably the team looks to see which categories got the most votes/comments. However, what happens is they say, "Oh, that topic got 64%, so that's got be a top priority for everyone." Everyone? There's 36% of the staff that indicated they didn't need it, so now it's a priority for everyone? This is not an effective strategy.

The Professionally Driven model targets the individual educator. If there is more than one teacher that is interested in the same topic, then they can form their own small group of learners. As such, small groups are formed naturally rather than being designated based on content areas or grade levels. This increases the likelihood of having an impact in the classroom.

3. LITTLE EFFECT ON THE CLASSROOM

Most traditional professional development, or even slight variations like the "a la carte" style, statistically have very little effect on classroom instructional change. This is either because teachers are not intrinsically motivated to begin integrating their new knowledge or because they simply see no value in the new information, feeling it doesn't apply to their instructional needs. Sometimes, administrators will put in place "accountability pieces" to ensure that teachers are at least trying the new methods. Teachers will usually comply, but in very few cases does it stick. As a result, traditional PD fails to transfer results to the classroom.

With the Professionally Driven model of personalized PD, integrating new strategies is encouraged and supported. This gives us a much higher chance of having an effect on learner outcomes.

4. LITTLE EFFECT ON LEARNER OUTCOMES

Because traditional professional development allows for very little transfer to the classroom, it therefore has virtually no effect on learner outcomes. If it's not integrated with fidelity, then how can the learners benefit from the new instructional strategies? For me, this is the biggest heartbreak of traditional PD. In his article *Staff Development and the Process of Teacher Change (1986)*, Thomas Guskey reminds us that the sole purpose of professional development is to have a **positive effect on learner outcomes**. In most cases of traditional PD, we don't even get the chance to see if the effects are positive or negative, because very few new instructional methods make it into classroom practice. It's my belief that some teachers are afraid to incorporate new instructional strategies at the risk of having them fail. I was guilty of this early on in my teaching career.

I vividly remember attempting to revamp the recreational reading program in my classroom. I wanted to use strategies to foster intrinsic motivation rather than using traditional "accountability" methods that have been proven to extinguish students' desires to read at the middle school level. After implementing the strategies, that fall I got the reading scores back from our state standardized test and found that many students' scores had declined from the previous year. The results were handed out at a whole staff PD, and I remember feeling absolutely embarrassed in front of my colleagues, who could see the same scores I was looking at.

I had my own data that I was collecting, though, that proved my students were reading more, but the scores measured something else and the whole experience made me question whether my methods were working. I spent time debating if I should go back to having students take quizzes after they read each book, but I couldn't convince myself that was the right way to build recreational reading. I ended up continuing my methods with some slight tweaking, and the following year saw much better results in all areas of reading. However, it's these negative experiences with scores that can really create a fixed mindset for teachers not wanting to try new methods. I know I was reluctant to try new methods after that, but I eventually got over this fear after sticking to my new methods and seeing the reading scores improve.

5. TEACHERS FEEL IT'S "ANOTHER THING"

This is perhaps the biggest reason why traditional professional development does not work. In reference to "yearly initiatives," teachers often say to me, "It feels like just one more thing added to my plate." Remember the bucket brigade analogy I mentioned earlier? Teachers are the last ones to receive the "water of knowledge." Every yearly initiative feels like another bucket being dumped on them. Or if we are to use the "plate" metaphor, yearly initiatives feel like nothing more than someone leading them down the buffet line and adding another food item to their plate...whether they like that food item or not. The problem is, teachers don't know what to do with the onslaught of excess food, so they simply reject it or push it to the side. From my own personal experience, professional development materials usually found their way into the recycling bin once the next initiative was introduced.

Teachers already experience the pressures of parents, grading, and extracurricular responsibilities, and adding more to their plates only causes unnecessary stress and anxiety. None of this will lead to a *change in teacher beliefs*. In my Professionally Driven model, instead of asking teachers to add to their plate, I ask them to **replace** something that isn't quite working with something better. I will discuss this idea and how it's a better use of time later in this book.

6. NEEDS MORE TIME

When attempting to shift an entire staff's instructional practice, I often hear the comparison of turning around the Titanic: both processes are very, *VERY* slow. If I am looking to shift my entire staff to, for example, Project-Based Learning and provide them the appropriate training, getting the entire staff to integrate this method with fidelity would take much longer than working with small groups of teachers who see the value in that new learning and believe that it can have a positive effect on learner outcomes. Simply put, shifting an entire staff on a single initiative can take years.

In contrast, personalized PD helps smaller groups to build intrinsic motivation and make the necessary moves for effective instruction more quickly. Rather than moving everyone in the same direction on a specific topic, personalized PD allows the topics to be determined by the educators, so long as the topics contain the same instructional goal: *positive effect on learner outcomes.*

7. SHORT-TERM EFFECTS.

If traditional professional development does produce some kind of effect on classroom instruction, more often than not that effect is short-term. This is usually because of an accountability piece built-in to ensure that the teacher is integrating it. The idea of accountability is inherently tied to extrinsic motivational practices. I talk more at length about the idea of "accountability" and my disdain for it later. With traditional professional development, the teacher is not intrinsically motivated to integrate strategies with fidelity.

Personalized PD offers effects that are much more long-term. Because the intrinsic motivation is built-in, teachers are more inclined to stick with it until it works.

As I reflected on my conversation that day at the table with the PD planning committee at Oelwein, my attempt to answer Mr. Westerberg's initial question—*What about them?*—only prompted a slew of more questions. However, these were important questions. They shaped the model that this book is all about.

All the pieces included in this model and in this book are my attempt to answer those original questions and others that I often hear when I present this particular model of personalized PD that allows *all* educators to truly be professionally driven. What does professionally driven mean to you? When I ask you to describe to me an educator that is professionally driven, what kind of educator do you imagine? Did a certain person or people come to mind? What if we could encourage *every* educator to be that kind of person?

With this book, I wish to provide everything a school district needs to feel confident in successfully implementing a model of personalized PD that adult learners *want* and *use* because they feel *empowered* to drive their own learning.

Like all conversations that revolve around something new or different, it's important to set up the WHY in chapters 2, 3, and 4. In my conversations with educators, it's easy to explain the model and *HOW* to set it up, but it's the conversations around the *WHY* that ultimately start to shift their mindsets from *passive learner* to *active learner*. This also initiates the conversation around how educators can develop their own growth mindset, not just students.

CHAPTER 2
GROWTH MINDSET AND PROFESSIONAL DEVELOPMENT

If we want students to develop a growth mindset and believe
they can learn anything, then we need educators who believe
the same for themselves.

If we know that traditional forms of PD are not conducive for all adult learners, then we have to begin to look at what does work. *Growth mindset*, a term coined by Carol Dweck in her book *Mindset: The New Psychology of Success (2007)*, is a term becoming more and more ubiquitous throughout academia and stands in contrast to another term coined by Dweck: **fixed mindset**. Those who haven't read the book may consider **growth mindset** nothing more than the latest buzzword circling the corridors of education. However, Dweck's work proves one thing: our belief in our ability to learn is the root for all other thinking that follows, and this belief *can* be developed.

Dweck, a professor at Stanford University, used two controlled groups of 5th graders compiled from various classrooms across the nation. All 5th graders were given the same baseline mental task that was designed to be completable by all of them. Once the students completed the mental task, half the group was praised with "Great job. You must be really smart at stuff like this." The second group was praised with "Great job. You must have worked really hard at completing that." While one group was praised for their perceived natural abilities, the other was praised for the effort that was put forth in attempting to complete the task.

After the completion of the first mental task, the students were then given a much harder task, one they were unlikely to complete. The group that was praised on their abilities gave up on the task far sooner than the group that was praised for their effort. After this seemingly impossible mental task, the two groups of students were given a choice. They could choose a task that would be considered much easier, like the first task they were asked to complete, or they could choose one that would be a little easier but still challenging to complete. The majority of students who were praised on their abilities chose the much simpler task, while the second group chose the more challenging task. While this may seem to be enough to prove that our approach to praise is essential in developing a growth mindset, Dweck took it further.

As a final task, all of the students were given a problem that could be easily solved, much like the very first task given. In this final task, however, students that were praised for their abilities did *worse* than their original scoring while the second group, praised for effort, scored *higher* than originally. This proves that developing a growth mindset is essential and foundational for long-term learning.

Dweck's work is so rudimentary, readers have applied her work to other areas and seen great success. Trevor Ragan (@train_ugly), founder of Train Ugly, helps athletic teams and coaches apply Dweck's work to their training regiments. A few years ago, he was asked by the USA Women's Volleyball team to reshape their training program. Trevor isn't a volleyball coach, but they didn't ask him to apply technique and skills. Instead, he looked at the areas in which they train and suggested ways in which to promote the mindset that "mistakes will be made, and we can learn from them." Every day, the team would list on their writable board what skills they felt were most difficult and were hoping to fail in attempting. The idea was that the faster we fail, the faster we get feedback, and the faster we can address our weakness and begin the work of turning it into a strength. According to Ragan, "USA Volleyball is the best I've seen at implementing growth mindset into their culture, and I've been lucky enough to watch them in action and collaborate and share ideas about the best ways to apply the research in a group setting." The belief that they could turn weaknesses into strengths ultimately led to their first ever world title in 2014. *But how do you establish that belief that it is truly something that can be developed?*

Another example that could give us some insight as to how we may develop this belief is Google X. One mode of learning I like to take advantage while I'm driving is podcasts. The TED Radio Hour is one that I have always appreciated, as it often tackles an overarching theme, bringing together several individual TED Talks related to one another in order to demonstrate one conclusive idea. In August of 2016, I was on my way to a Character Counts Conference to host a session on how to build a child's character by helping them develop their growth mindset. I was excited for the 75 minute drive, because there was a new TED Radio Hour podcast episode that had just come out entitled, "Failure is an Option." It was perfect timing, given that it related to what I had planned to cover in my session.

There was one particular TED Talk highlighted, though, that I found to be especially intriguing. It discussed a facility owned by Google called Google X. This facility contains some very big thinkers who seek out problems in the world and then think outside the box to try to solve them. Google Glass is one product that came out of Google X. Some may remember its short stint in society as the glasses that can take pictures, video, and use the lenses to overlay augmented information on top of a current view of the user's environment. Google Glass did not become the take-off product that Google was hoping for. While some may have seen the product's great potential, it ultimately wasn't socially acceptable to wear a cellphone on your face because many were concerned with privacy. You could never tell if someone wearing Google Glasses was taking a photo or recording you; a cellphone is less discrete. It was a flop in the eyes of society, but not to Google.

At Google X, they handle the idea of failure similarly to that of the U.S. Women's Volleyball Team. When a team project fails at Google X, the manager brings the team up in front of all the other employees and publicly recognizes their failure in their attempt to solve a big problem. The manager then announces that each member of the team will be receiving a bonus. Yes, you read that right. While every other major company that we know of hands out bonuses to those who reach a target number designated as successful in the company's eyes, Google X awards failures in the attempt of success. While most reward the final *product*, Google X rewards the *process*, and by overtly focusing on process, Google X emphasizes the potential for growth. It's this focus that develops a growth mindset.

As soon as I got to the conference that day, I added a link to the podcast in my presentation, because there were several valuable takeaways related to the idea of growth mindset.

The idea of failure is a central point that is brought up over and over again when it comes to growth or fixed mindsets. It is a prevalent theme, and our approach to it helps us to determine which mindset we currently reside in. Before digging into the differences between growth and fixed mindset individuals, I think it's important to first reacquaint ourselves with the idea of *fear*.

At its core, fear is what triggers the physiological reaction of *fight-or-flight*. In 1932, physiologist Walter Cannon coined this phrase to describe the natural reaction of self-preservation when an animal feels threatened, including humans. *But what does this look like specifically for educators in an academic setting?* This moment of fear plays a huge role in determining whether we are currently operating with a fixed mindset or a growth mindset. Take a look at the differences between the two mindsets, according to Dweck.

Fixed Mindset	Mindset Characteristics	Growth Mindset
Set - you have what you're born with	**Skills & Abilities**	Can grow and be developed
Not looking bad	**Main Concern**	Learning, growing, improving
Something you do when you're not good	**Effort**	An important part of learning
Give up & check out	**Challenges**	Persevere and work through them
Hate making them & try to avoid making them	**Mistakes**	Treat them as a learning opportunity
Take it personally /get defensive	**Feedback**	Like it and use it

I'm sure as you read through these, you were able to picture certain people with each characteristic. Were you able to picture yourself? When I work with educators and focus on their learning, in most cases, I look at the **Main Concern** and **Feedback** categories. *Is the educator afraid to look inferior in front of their students or colleagues?*

How do they typically react when receiving feedback from their students or colleagues? If you are already picturing someone with a fixed mindset when I ask those two questions, there is something you should keep in mind: we move freely from fixed to growth mindset on a spectrum, not a light switch. That means there is distance to be gained in *several* steps in either direction between the two ends of the spectrum. We do not move from fixed mindset to growth mindset in a single step. For some, the movement might be slow, and for others it might be quicker. It is important to remember that we can move in either direction. The question, then, that must be asked is, *What affects the movement?*

THE PROCESS OF MOVING MINDSETS

The process of moving in either direction begins with being immersed in a fight-or-flight situation. We first have to be placed in that moment of uncomfortableness and uncertainty in order to gauge our physiological response triggered by the amygdala in our brain. When it comes to our own learning as adult educators, that moment could arise from a variety of things: our comfort level with technology use, our content knowledge of our subject matter, our knowledge of pedagogical strategies, or a host of other situations. In most cases, it's going to be triggered by the feeling of *I don't know*, because as educators, we feel we *ought* to know.

Once we have experienced that fight-or-flight situation—either intentionally or unintentionally—it is then that we are capable of being nudged in either mindset direction. This nudge might come from another colleague, a parent, an instructional coach, or even our students. If we are faced with a situation of *I don't know*, and someone says to us, "It's OK not to know," then we are more likely to move in the direction of the growth mindset and see the *I don't know* as part of the process. If we're told, "Well, you should know," and made to feel inferior, then we're shoved in the direction of a fixed mindset where we become concerned with how we look in front of others, particularly in terms of intelligence. With each fight-or-flight moment we experience thereafter, we are more inclined to take the road we took before. We either flee or avoid the situation because of a reinforced fear of looking inferior, or we develop a formidable grit to persevere and learn. This will also have a significant impact on the second category that often applies to educators: **feedback**.

CHOOSING FIGHT

Once educators have been nudged in either mindset direction, their response to feedback becomes directly affected. The further they move towards a growth mindset, the more open they are to feedback, even so far as to request it. In contrast, when moved towards a fixed mindset concerned with looking inferior, feedback from others is avoided, and when given, received defensively.

I have experienced this as a consultant/coach from time to time. It's difficult sometimes to work through those moments, and the worst thing I can do is continue with the feedback. The educator has shut down. They don't want to hear it. Continuing is futile. However, I have to be cognizant that they have been *conditioned* into this fixed mindset. I have to realize they are tired of having someone else tell them what isn't working and offer to have them add their own voice, asking instead, "What do you feel could be working better? What support do you need from me?" This is a much more empathetic approach, and I have seen educators begin to at least drop some walls. They may not be moving towards a growth mindset **yet** (another keyword that Dweck says is crucial for developing a growth mindset), but we've opened the lines of communication. So, the next time they are in a fight-or-flight situation, they might be willing to listen to me when I say to them, "It's OK not to know," and know that I mean it when I say it, thus beginning the nudge towards a growth mindset.

ONLY A GROWTH MINDSET CAN EMPOWER A GROWTH MINDSET

It takes someone who possesses a growth mindset in order to empower others to become the same. However, there is a growing trend that is highly discouraging to me and needs to stop immediately. I keep my finger on the pulse of education mainly through the largest discussion platform for educators: Twitter. (In fact, I try to include the Twitter handles of those mentioned in this book in parentheses behind their name in order to encourage you to go and connect with them.) There are literally hundreds of Twitter chats about education and all aspects of it every week. I try to partake in or at least follow a few different ones from time to time in order to gain a sense of the current attitudes of teachers and administrators, particularly those passionate about the state of learning in our educational systems.

While I encounter positive attitudes from most on Twitter about the importance of helping students no matter what, I can't say the same attitudes have been expressed towards educators. There is a notion out there that teachers are being separated into two categories: those that take the initiative to continue learning and those that are too "lazy" to do so. Attached to this idea is a follow-up: "lazy" teachers need to leave the profession. This seems to be a very fixed mindset approach. Rather than figuring out how to empower, we should simply remove the "bad apples."

I thought this belief was supported by just a few misguided individuals that existed outside of the teaching profession. Nope. These are other teachers and administrators saying this aloud on a social media platform that is open to the world, and it is definitely more than just one individual. I see this message expressed at least a few times a month by a variety of people involved in education. I thought to myself, *Well, this is just Twitter. Does anyone really listen to those saying these things on Twitter?* I still refused to believe that educators really had this fixed mindset and felt this way until I heard a keynote speaker say at a conference in front of hundreds of educators, "There are great teachers out there, and there are loser teachers who just don't take initiative to be great. If you have a teacher who wants to leave the profession, then don't stop them." My jaw dropped in absolute disbelief. Here was a very, and I mean very, well-known keynote speaker who has published over a dozen books, not necessarily calling for the active exodus of "lazy" teachers, but saying we shouldn't stop it either.

If you are one that feels the same way as this keynote speaker or the dozens of others that I see on Twitter and claim to be of a growth mindset when it comes to learning, you are absolutely fooling yourself. This thinking says, *You are either a great teacher or a lousy one, and lousy ones* **choose** *not to be great.* It implies that an educator can flip a switch in their thinking: be *great* or be *lousy*, it's your choice. But remember, our mindset is not a switch, especially when we have been conditioned into a fixed mindset through traditional forms of professional development. This kind of thinking also places full responsibility on the educator, not on the others that may have contributed to the fixed mindset. It's no different than a student who has been conditioned to think, *What's the point of school?* when they have been treated like a failure time and time again.

In any process worth tackling, including learning, students *and* educators will automatically feel like failures when they don't get the results they are hoping for in those moments of fight-or-flight. This feeling happens naturally, with no assistance from others. They may have taken the risk to fight, but encountered a mistake and all by themselves triggered the feeling of failure. However, it's that outside voice that can influence them to see the failure as a lesson in a process or the final product. *If we are expected to stick with the students and continue to help them see the lesson in every failure, then why do we not have the same expectations for ourselves or our educational colleagues?*

TURNING CATERPILLARS INTO BUTTERFLIES

I have had the opportunity to take part in the Authentic Intellectual Work (AIW) training in order to become a lead coach. AIW is a framework that helps educators put a direct focus on the effectiveness of instruction through a process of scoring teacher tasks, student work, and teacher instruction in collaborative groups. I don't need to go into much detail, but the reason I mention AIW is because in that training, there was a very powerful metaphor used that I feel really expresses how we need to approach every learner, both student and adult.

The trainers spoke about how all learners are like caterpillars. If you dissect a caterpillar directly down the middle, you can see wings that are forming on the inside. This really spoke to me, and I try to keep it in the forefront of my mind when I approach any learner, including myself. I absolutely refuse to label teachers as lousy or lazy, but instead I say to myself, *They are just a caterpillar still. How can I help them transition into that butterfly?* Waving to them in relief as they walk out the door certainly isn't the way. If it can't be done with a student, then it shouldn't be allowed as an option for adults either. I had a colleague reply that this metaphor only works with caterpillars and that sometimes it feels that you're dealing with a cockroach. But I would argue that some of the best mentors/coaches can make any cockroach feel like a caterpillar with the potential to be a butterfly.

Through our mentoring and coaching, we can encourage ourselves and our fellow educators to take *instructional* risks just as we encourage students to take *learning* risks. But what does it mean to take an instructional risk? Does it mean to try a new tech tool in the classroom? If working with technology is a personal fight-or-flight situation, then perhaps. However, I would argue that there is an even greater risk that we can take as educators: owning up to weaknesses in our instruction and working to make them better. This is also where we see the biggest gains in our own growth mindset. If I personally go through the active process of turning a weakness into a strength, I will understand more deeply that my instruction is malleable, just like the skills I acquire and my own mindset.

STRENGTHS BORN FROM WEAKNESSES

This idea of focusing on weaknesses and working to morph them into strengths is found in many sports, but I've never heard it spoken of more directly and explicitly than in CrossFit, a sport that started in 2000 in Santa Cruz, California, and has quickly become the fastest growing sport worldwide. Now, I can already imagine the eye-rolling by those who are tired of listening to protein powder pushers pontificating about muscle-ups, power cleans, and WODs (Workout of the Day). I'm not asking anyone to go out and *do* CrossFit, but I would suggest you watch any of the re-runs from the CrossFit Games on CrossFit's YouTube channel. The CrossFit community itself takes great pride in testing fitness in order to expose weaknesses. In fact, that's one of its main objectives.

In 2015, CrossFit Games Director Dave Castro, who develops the workouts that the athletes must complete, incorporated a new movement that had not been seen in the Games before: the peg board. Imagine the peg boards that you would often see in schools around the 1980's but 30 feet in height. Athletes needed to complete three ascents in conjunction with another fitness movement, all for the fastest time. Since the athletes had already completed eight previous events over the course of four days prior to this particular one, the majority of the athletes couldn't complete the three ascents.

Some criticized Castro and the CrossFit Games for including an exercise that had not been a part of any training regiment in CrossFit. How could athletes perform a task that they did not know of ahead of time? Still, in 2016, the peg board was brought back in one of the latter events on the final day of competition once again. Castro's reasoning? "The purpose of CrossFit is to not allow yourself to plateau, but continually challenge yourself. In 2015, we found a weakness for a lot of these athletes. What better way to test if you've gotten better than to include it again this year?" And in 2016, more athletes were able to complete the peg board, including those athletes that failed to do so the previous year. This aligns very well with the quote by fitness guru Fred Devito and now mantra for many in fitness, "If it doesn't challenge you, it won't change you."

What also makes CrossFit unique is that they are intentionally testing fitness with the intent to expose weaknesses *in front of a world audience*. This may sound demented and cruel, and to the majority of people, it sounds like a living nightmare: looking inferior in front of others. But the idea is, *How are we supposed to get better at anything unless we discover what it is we're not good at?* I have watched the CrossFit Games online for five years now, and you can find failed attempts by individuals in almost every event. However, after each failed attempt, they are taking mental notes as to what weaknesses are being exposed. They put those on the brain-shelf and revisit them once training kicks in for the next season.

Some athletes qualify for the CrossFit Games one year, then fail to qualify the next year. Samantha Briggs stood on top of the podium at the CrossFit Games in 2013 in the Individual Women category but failed to even qualify the following year. This is similar to educators when we experience a very challenging year (behavior, test scores, etc.) We can very easily point the blame at students, or worse yet, let the idea of failing take over and consider leaving the classroom. However, Briggs has developed a growth mindset. While some would throw their hands up and quit the sport, she simply approached it as, "I have a lot of work to do for next year." And in 2015, 2016, and 2017, Briggs was back at the CrossFit Games competing for that top spot.

I love having my three kids watch the CrossFit Games with me. I especially like the interviews with athletes after each event. My kids get to hear athletes explicitly say, "Last year (X) was a major weakness. This last year, I did (X) at least every week in order to get better." Over and over you hear athletes fill in (X) with any variety of CrossFit movements they identified as a weakness. One athlete in particular, Mat Fraser, finished runner-up in 2014 and 2015. In 2016, he stood on top of the podium in dominating fashion with the most margin of win by any athlete before, including the previous four-time champion Rich Froning. Mat is a man of few words, but in his interview after the last event, he was asked what the difference in his training was that year. His reply? "I really worked to address any weakness I had that prevented me from winning the last two years. I was relentless in making sure they would be strengths for me this year and not hold me back." He also mentioned in his interview that he was disappointed one of his weaknesses from the previous year, tire flipping, was not included in that year's Games, because he was looking forward to demonstrating how much he had improved. These are people who thrive at the opportunity to prove that they have gotten better from one year to the next.

My kids, the oldest being nine years old, get to visually see the growth mindset in full form when they watch the CrossFit Games. They get to see people (mainly adults) tested, fail, acknowledge their specific shortcomings, and work to turn them into strengths. This is, I believe, the formula in changing fixed mindset to growth mindset. If we see others go through this process, we are more inclined to go through it as well. We also get to see those that have turned weaknesses into strengths being praised for the work they have put in year after year. *How are students in your building seeing the adult learners go through a similar process? Is the process of turning weaknesses into strengths being modeled for your students?*

CrossFit is constantly sharing videos that show various athletes doing the daily workouts and either crushing it or struggling through it. My kids get to see the struggle, the process, the journey of each athlete as they train and attempt to qualify for the Games. The struggle and training is not kept secret, but rather, CrossFit puts a direct light on it. It's this acute focus on the process and growth from weakness to strength that develops one's growth mindset. To reference back to Devito's quote, "If it doesn't challenge you, it won't change you," he is essentially saying that identifying *strengths* and working to make them stronger does *not* change us. We have to identify the weaknesses in order to see growth.

In contrast to CrossFit, the Olympics is an athletic event that doesn't contribute to a growth mindset for those watching. Rarely do we get to see the struggle that Olympic athletes go through in order to attain that gold medal. Sure, we see the backstories for some, but what we ultimately see is the pressure to be perfect in Olympic performance: the final product. Mistakes are penalized. We see a focus on natural ability, like Usian Bolt's long legs that allow him to take fewer steps than most runners, or Michael Phelps' long torso that may give him slight mechanical advantages when it comes to swimming. This type of focus projects a fixed mindset to the viewers.

GETTING GRITTY

Growth mindset is perhaps most visible in athletics, but it can be seen everywhere. If you simply ask the question, *"Do you believe you can get better at (X)?"* You can replace (X) with almost anything, and you will discover what your mindset approach is toward that topic. For example, I have a growth mindset when it comes to *learning*, but my mindset is quite fixed when it comes to my thoughts on being a *marathon runner*. I look at my short legs and fast twitch muscles and convince myself that I'm not built for long distance running; I focus on my abilities, or lack thereof. But I also realize and acknowledge that my mindset is fixed when it comes to this topic, which is one of the first steps in shifting to a growth mindset. Our mindset differs from topic to topic, but as long as one can identify where it is fixed, one can identify the steps necessary to change it. This is applying the idea of **grit**.

Angela Duckworth (@angeladuckw) speaks of grit in her book *Grit: The Power of Passion and Perseverance* (2016). In her work, she accredits Dweck's work as a starting point for identifying where to apply grit. We cannot apply grit to a topic where we feel an innate strength or ability already exists. Grit can only be applied to an area that we feel is a weakness. It can be changed, but we have to believe it can be changed. I have to believe that I can run a marathon if I train hard enough, regardless of my physical circumstances, and after reading *Mindset* and *Grit*, I do believe I can run a marathon if I train enough. I may not have the fastest time, but I know I can at least finish. This is because I've learned to stop focusing on the product and instead focus on the process.

An additional contribution to my shift in thinking was watching my wife complete a half marathon, and she's never even run a 5K. She very much doubted her own abilities to do so until some of her friends trained for the same half marathon the year before. I got to watch her struggle through her training and see the process it took. I was also able to watch the final product. To me, this is one example of when we see others struggle through a process, rather than just viewing the final product, we are innately invited to do the same. When we see someone realize they had wings forming on the inside, and take notice of the transition, we begin to realize that we have the same abilities. Moreover, whether I decide to run or not, my confidence in my ability to complete a full marathon has strengthened.

FROM POINT A TO POINT B

Maybe the word **weakness** still doesn't settle well with you even after all the examples I've given. Maybe you prefer to call it something else, such as "area of potential growth." Either way, we are merely trying to label Point A on the journey. And, in order to complete a journey, we also need to identify Point B. You can label these two points anything that resonates with you, but the most important part of this whole equation is the path between Point A and Point B. The path may be long, winding, and loop back a few times, but it's important nonetheless.

When I think of someone who is professionally driven, I picture someone who embraces the word *weakness* and doesn't shy away from it. They may even actively seek out their own weaknesses, because they know it's just Point A and that Point B is strength. They may not know the exact path between those two points, but the thought of going on that journey excites and invigorates them. They don't see weakness as unchangeable or as something that defines them. In fact, they refuse to let it define them. That's why they become driven to change it. But by all means, label Point A and Point B however you wish, so long as you are driven to embark on that path between the two.

So, if we know that a growth mindset is foundational when it comes to learning, it is no surprise that it should also be applied to facilitating learning. That is to say, we all have weaknesses as educators, but we can work to turn our weaknesses into strengths. The problem is identifying which weakness to focus on first. We may have weaknesses when it comes to classroom management or organization, but I would argue that these weaknesses shouldn't be focused on first. As educators, we need to spend our professional development time focusing on learnings that put the students first. We need to define the purpose of professional development.

THE PURPOSE OF PD

It didn't take long for me to experience traditional professional development before I began to ask myself, *Why do we even do PD?* In Iowa, one of our state teaching standards is *Engages in professional growth.* I would imagine that most, if not all states have a standard similar to this one. So the answer to my question could be...*because we have to*, and unfortunately this might be how PD is viewed and treated. However, it's the work of Thomas Guskey, *Professional Development and Teacher Change* (1986), that better lays out for us the *why* behind the process educators must go through in order to change their instructional practice and beliefs. This is a process that my Professionally Driven model attempts to move educators through in order to improve their instructional practices and positively affect learner outcomes.

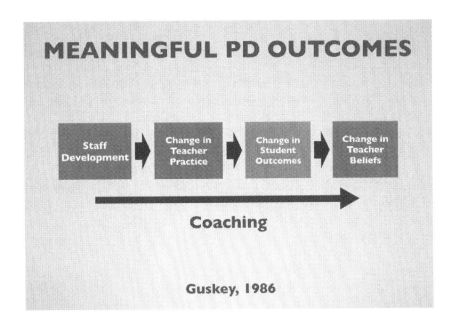

1. **Staff Development**: This is the traditional professional development that teachers usually receive in order to further their own knowledge when it comes to instructional practices. It's the *what-teachers-don't-know* part that I hear a lot of administrators talk about. This is simply the gathering of new information. How that's done can vary.

2. **Change in Teacher Practice**: Once a teacher gathers new knowledge in the staff development phase, it should lead to an instructional change in their classroom practices. If we were to apply this same thinking to *all* roles in education including the administrators and instructional coaches, we could amend the word *teacher* with ***educator*** and *classroom* with ***learning environment***.

3. **Change in Student Outcomes**: If an educator identifies an instructional weakness and works to change that weakness, then a change should be seen in student outcomes. However, I would argue that the change must be a *positive* one. If what I am attempting to do in my classroom is having a *negative* effect on student outcomes, I should refocus my efforts. Also, I would amend the word *student* to ***learner***. This allows administrators and instructional coaches to move through the same process. It doesn't matter what role you play in education, you should be able to identify *Who are my learners?*

4. **Change in Teacher Beliefs**: If I have followed the previous three phases correctly and have seen a positive effect on learner outcomes, then my own teaching beliefs about my instruction will change for the better. And in this phase, we could once again amend the word *teacher* for ***educator***.

We can clearly see that Guskey's process visually lays out how to move from a fixed to growth mindset when it comes to our own learning as educators. His last step says it all, after some amending: "Change in *Educator* Beliefs." Guskey's model also identifies that in order to move the highest percentage of educators through all four phases, **coaching** is required. It's that extra layer of in-house support that educators need when they feel stuck in the process. My Professionally Driven model relies on an instructional coach or some other coaching role. Just as teachers are the support for learning in their classrooms, instructional coaches are the support for learning in the district. How the specific role of coach is utilized within this Professionally Driven model will be discussed in Chapter 6.

For some, moving through this process makes a lot of sense and seems doable. The part where nearly every educator gets hung up, though, is in finding their weakness. We cannot start this journey without knowing even where to start. We need to have something definitive, not a process of random selection. We also can't have educators whimsically choosing a weakness based on something they feel they don't know enough about. "I don't know enough about (X), and I want to learn more" is *not* a weakness. There are many things in this world that we know little about, but that doesn't necessarily constitute them as weaknesses. If that were the case, an educator could go on Twitter and find an educational topic they may know hardly anything about and choose to focus on that. While this isn't a bad thing, it doesn't follow our overarching question: **What will have a positive effect on learner outcomes?** This is our Point B, the summit of our journey, if you will. Therefore, we must concretely determine what Point A is at the foot of the mountain. This is our weakness worth tackling first.

So when it comes to education and learning, how do we identify that weakness that we should focus on first? Fortunately, there are models out there that do a great job of this. Your school may be implementing one right now. As I mentioned before, I have been involved with the training for Authentic Intellectual Work (AIW). By scoring instructional tasks, student work, and live instruction, teachers generate objective conversations about the rigor and instructional value of learning. I have talked with other trainers, teachers, and coaches that are involved with AIW, and they really like that it helps to concretely identify where their instruction is weak. I, too, have experienced this within scoring sessions.

Many schools also use Professional Learning Communities (PLC) as a way of organizing teacher collaboration and conversations around student data. Through this work, teachers are able to identify data that points to potential instructional weaknesses. However, in many of the schools I work with, teachers report that PLC's seem to work well at the elementary grade levels, but they're not sure how effective it is at the secondary level. This isn't criticizing the idea of

PLC's or a school's implementation of them, I just think teachers are saying, "So, we see the data...now what?"

Your school may be using a different model or framework to foster teacher collaboration and look critically at data, and I support any that does this. However, I would like to offer another strategy that I have used that seems to resonate with educators at all levels.

IDENTIFYING THE WEAK SPOT

I know it can be difficult for some to identify that they have a weak spot in their instruction. However, I believe I have already laid out all the reasons why I absolutely insist on referencing it as a **weak spot** and not sugar-coating it with any other term. I have seen admins and coaches squirm or cringe at the idea of addressing it as a weak spot and attempt to change it to a lighter term. But if we want to take all educators through the process of developing their own growth mindset, we must first let them see that it's OK to be imperfect and to have weaknesses. As mentioned before, this is also a crucial step in helping them know where to apply grit. We should use this terminology because we are offering a specific method to turn that weakness into a strength. We're not leaving them high and dry and saying, "You have a weakness as an educator. Now figure out how to fix it." We're providing the support necessary to give educators the confidence to try and fail forward on their journey. Eventually, they will get there, and we need to let them know that. We are supporting a process of *replacing*, not *adding*.

In my first two years as a consultant, working with hundreds of teachers in my part of the state, I can say with confidence that the #1 comment I hear from teachers regarding PD is "We don't want another thing added to our plate!" They say this vehemently to administrators and even to me...and I agree with them. I was feeling the same way just a few years before. I quickly learned that we have to stop letting PD feel like it's another thing being added, and I think identifying a weak spot helps. I try to tell educators that when we identify their weak spot, essentially what I am asking them to do is identify what is currently not working with their classroom instruction. Then, as we progress through the Professionally Driven model, I'm simply asking them to research strategies that would work better, replacing those weak strategies with stronger, more effective ones. This way, nothing is being added to their plate, but rather we are attempting to *replace* the bad stuff with better stuff.

The idea of *replacing* vs. *adding* is much more appealing to educators, and as a result, they are far more inclined to acknowledge their weak spots. Not only that, when educators identify their weaknesses themselves, they are less likely to become defensive, unlike when an administrator or outside expert comes in and identifies it for them. *So, how do we identify what is considered ineffective classroom instruction?* Allow me to reacquaint you with Mr. Benjamin Bloom.

LOWER-LEVELS TO UPPER-LEVELS

Every educator is familiar with Bloom's taxonomy. It comes up in college teacher prep programs all across the nation. However, most teachers become unfamiliar with it very quickly when they begin teaching inside the classroom. This, of course, is at no fault of the teacher. As soon as the reality of having 25-30 students hits, we tend to lose sight of those learning models that we covered in our methods courses in college. I was one of those teachers that spent the first few years just trying to survive. I, too, needed to be reacquainted with Bloom's taxonomy. It wasn't until I saw Lorin Anderson's revised version of Bloom's taxonomy

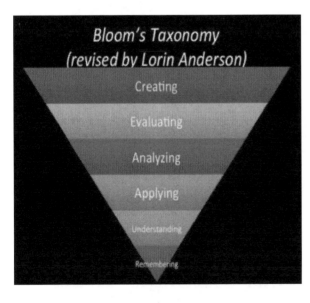

Bloom's Taxonomy
(revised by Lorin Anderson)

Creating
Evaluating
Analyzing
Applying
Understanding
Remembering

that I realized exactly where I was going wrong with it all. I began to identify my own weaknesses in my instruction.

In the original version of Bloom's taxonomy, the pyramid is fairly traditional. The lowest levels of thinking are the largest and form the solid foundation for the upper levels of thinking. However, the original version is slightly misleading, visually speaking. If the size of the level is in relation to the amount of time in class that students should be spending there, then it appears that a student should be thinking in the lower-levels for the majority of their learning experience. We know that this is highly ineffective. This is where we see a lot of classroom management issues occur as well.

When students are cognitively disengaged, they will find other ways of re-engaging themselves. Students will quickly begin to perceive the content as "boring" and disengage with it. In our first year of going 1:1 with iPads in my school district, some teachers were quickly becoming frustrated with the number of students that were being caught watching YouTube videos in class instead of doing what had been assigned. One teacher wanted YouTube blocked, but my reply was, "If students find YouTube more engaging than my lesson, then there's a problem with my lesson...not YouTube."

In Lorin Anderson's revised version of Bloom's taxonomy, the pyramid is flipped. This better represents the amount of time that students should be spending at each level of learning and thinking. We want students to be more actively involved with the upper levels of thinking (Analyze, Evaluate, and Create). Not only that, we want them up there as frequently as possible and for the longest duration of time. This is how we *cognitively engage* students and maximize their learning opportunities.

I too often hear the word "engagement" used by teachers, administrators, and even well-known keynote speakers with multiple books published (yes, the same one I mentioned before). The word is used differently every time. Does engagement mean 25-30 sets of eyes looking at me? Does it mean students being physically active and/or talking? Does it mean they are being entertained? I argue, no. Engagement does not equate to "paying attention." And too many educators mistaken *engaged* with "entertained." There are thousands of tools to make the lower-levels of learning more entertaining, but that doesn't mean it makes content more cognitively engaging if all the students are doing is *remembering*, *understanding*, or *applying*.

The goal of teaching should be to have learners *analyzing, evaluating*, and *creating* as frequently as possible and for the longest duration of time during the class time that I have with them. I often use the following equation with educators to sum up my definition.

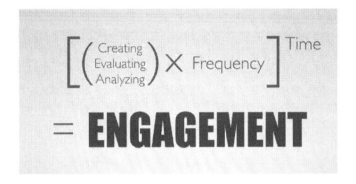

$$\left[\begin{pmatrix} \text{Creating} \\ \text{Evaluating} \\ \text{Analyzing} \end{pmatrix} \times \text{Frequency} \right]^{\text{Time}}$$

$$= \textbf{ENGAGEMENT}$$

Initially, I had the equation being divided by *Time* to visually represent the idea of "over time," but a colleague of mine, Jason Martin-Hiner (@jmartinhiner), our Science consultant, corrected my math by pointing out that if I divided by *Time* I would actually have less engagement...mathematically. Coming from an English education background, it was a harmless mistake on my part, and he helped me to correct it by showing that it should be to the power of *Time*. While this may make less sense to me, I do want it to be more user-friendly for all.

So, what is the ultimate goal of this Professionally Driven model? The objective is for educators to self-identify where learners are frequently spending time in the lower levels of Bloom's taxonomy. This is the weak spot. It is then the educator's goal to move learners to the upper levels. This is the very process I had to use when I first started teaching.

JAROD'S STORY

When I first started my teaching career as a middle school and high school English teacher, vocabulary acquisition quickly became one of my weaknesses in instruction. Of course, as a first year teacher, I used a lot of what was given to me from the previous teacher. In this case, it was a retired teacher of 30+ years of teaching. The filing cabinets that sat stoically in the corner of my newly inherited classroom contained an entire drawer full of vocab packets. Each week's packet included 15 new vocabulary words. Those words, of course, had definitions and parts of speech that were then used to complete the rest of the packet. There were sections for matching, fill in the blank, multiple choice, and even a few short answers.

I would have students complete these packets every one to two weeks. Most of the students groaned about completing them, and at the time, I just thought they were being apathetic teenagers. However, looking back, I would have too. But perhaps the most discouraging part was when I would slip a vocab word into my other lessons and activities and none of the students would pick up on it. Even if I paused to see if it rang a bell with any of them, only one or two students might faintly recall the word. This is how I knew I needed to do something different. If I would have used Bloom's Taxonomy as my guide, I would have realized that my students were only reaching the Applying level.

In my second year, I discovered something online that I wholeheartedly thought would revolutionize vocabulary acquisition in my classroom: leveled vocabulary. There were separate vocabulary lists for each level. Level A contained easier words while Level Z contained higher, above grade level words. However, all levels were still accompanied by a packet. I was duped into thinking that this was great. *I could differentiate the vocabulary work, because students are working with vocabulary words at their level.* The problem was, though, all I differentiated was the **Applying** level. Students were still filling in blanks, matching, and giving short answers. It wasn't until I went back to Bloom's taxonomy did I realize that my students were never going above the Applying level...and that wasn't their fault.

I decided to scrap the vocabulary packets altogether, and I went back to the drawing board.

I realized that I needed to get students to actually use the vocabulary words, **creating** something with them in order to move into the upper levels of Bloom's taxonomy. Students would get 15 words, half of which were self-identified by them from the books and stories we read. Their only criteria was to create something with those 15 words based on the context of the definitions and without changing the part of speech. Every two weeks, we would do a different kind of project, eventually building up to their own choice in whatever they wanted to create. I had students that would use GarageBand to create an audio newscast or a rap. I had some students that wrote a script for a short skit that they would perform live in front of the class. I had some students create short videos, often parodies. I even had a few students that would create a separate Vine for each word and then put them all together; this was before I even knew what a Vine was. Soon enough, I had every student creating something using all 15 words correctly in whatever creative format they wish to use.

I knew this was more effective for two reasons: 1) students performed better on the quizzes and 2) students recognized the words when we used them in the classroom. I also had a fellow teacher come to me between class periods and ask if we had used a particular word that week for vocabulary. I told him that we had actually learned that word last month. He asked because he had five students use that word in their papers for his class.

This is also when I began to realize how to effectively integrate technology for the sake of learning. When I attempted to move students from lower-levels to upper-levels more frequently, nine times out ten, technology was involved (take another glance at the student vocab examples I listed above and see what I mean). This is when I realized that technology allowed me to move students to the upper-levels more efficiently and, as importantly, keep them there. I was never able to achieve this with a textbook or worksheet. I could have students do electronic worksheets, but it's where students are **cognitively operating** that matters most.

FINDING AND FILTERING THE WEAK SPOT

Allowing educators to be more cognizant of the weak spot in their instruction is critical when attempting to develop a growth mindset. It's a matter of encouraging them to seek out more effective strategies in order to have the greatest impact on learning. Notice I did *not* say, "We need to continually point out what educators could improve on." This does not make an educator more cognizant. I've been guilty of doing this myself, even with students.

To prepare educators for finding their own weak spots, I give a presentation similar to what I have just given you:

- Re-acquaint teachers with the revised version of Bloom's taxonomy.
- Tell my story of vocabulary acquisition.
- Present the equation that attempts to define cognitive engagement.

I then present two questions to the teachers:
1. Where do you see your students consistently operating in the lower levels of Bloom's taxonomy?
2. In that area, how can you move them into the upper levels more frequently?

These two questions can be applied to any teacher at any grade level over the course of their entire teaching career, because they will always have new learners year after year. The worldly context that students live in is continually changing, and ways of connecting content to worldly context will always need developing. We no longer teach in a time where content can remain static on a worksheet, packet, or textbook. This is essentially what every type of *Fill-in-the-Blank Learning* attempts to encourage teachers to do. From *Project-Based Learning* to *Blended Learning*, it's all about getting students into the upper-levels of Bloom's taxonomy more frequently and for a longer duration of time. Not only that, the second question will most likely put educators in an uncomfortable fight-or-flight moment: the "I don't know" moment.

However, once a teacher identifies what their instructional weakness is and decides on a topic/question that would make it better, I have three filters that I apply to determine whether or not that topic/question is *the* topic that they should be focusing on. These three filters are, perhaps, the most important part to identifying the weak spot.

1. Is the topic/question focused on having *positive effects on learner outcomes*? If yes, move to the 2nd filter.
2. Is the topic/question tool-driven? If no, and you still have more than one topic/question that you are looking to explore, then move to the 3rd filter.
3. Which topic/question are you most excited to tackle?

The first question I ask is merely there to make sure the focus is on the **student**. The second question is to ensure the focus is on **pedagogy**, not tools. When we kicked off the Professionally Driven model at Oelwein, I vividly remember going from group to group to check in and see what topics/questions were being tackled by educators. I saw two math teachers partnered up and looking as though they still weren't quite sure if their topic was appropriate or not. It was a look very similar to what I have seen with students. I walked over to them and simply posed the question, "What did you guys have in mind for your first journey?" They looked at each other for a moment before one replied, "We think we want to learn how to use Khan Academy." Immediately, in my mind, I knew that this didn't meet the 2nd filter. Rather than telling them "no," though, and explaining that they were thinking in the wrong direction, I simply asked, "Well, what is it you are hoping to achieve with Khan Academy?" Again, they looked at each other for a second or two. This time the other teacher replied, "I think we are looking to differentiate our math instruction more for our 8th graders."

By posing the question to them the way that I did, they were able to discover the true topic that they should be seeking. I said to them, "Explore *that* question, and you guys may find that Khan Academy is not the right tool based on your learners' needs and your teaching styles." In the process of growth, it can be tricky to stay on the intended path. It's OK to veer off at times. That's part of the learning process. However, re-adjusting might be necessary in order to get back on that right path and ultimately reach that final destination.

The third filter serves to ensure that **intrinsic motivation** is established right from the beginning. This is the focus in the next chapter.

The growth mindset is important for professionally driven educators to understand, not just for students' learning sake but for our own as well. It's what allows us to be vigilant of instructional weaknesses, so we may summon the grit and perseverance to turn them into strengths. Analyzing our instruction at this level will have the greatest impact on true cognitive engagement for students.

QUESTIONS TO CONSIDER FOR GROWTH MINDSET AND PROFESSIONAL DEVELOPMENT...

Before moving on to Chapter 3, I encourage you to reflect on these questions regarding growth mindset and the current form of professional development in your district:

1. What *instructional weaknesses* are holding you back from being the best educator you can be (whether you are a teacher, administrator, or another role in education)? What instructional weaknesses of yours are holding back students?
2. In your building/district, when educators identify instructional weaknesses, are they given the time and support to turn them into strengths? Or is it expected of them to work on this outside of their contract time?
3. How is *growth mindset* among adults currently being encouraged in your district, and not just talked about?
4. How are educators (including administrators) encouraged to take *instructional risks*?
5. When an educator fails, what is the response (if any) from others in the district? Do these responses promote a *fixed* or *growth* mindset?
6. What *support* is currently being provided for teachers in your district that make them feel comfortable taking risks if they choose to go on a learning journey?
7. Does your district tend to focus on the *process* or the *product*?
8. Do you currently provide *feedback* to adult learners that focuses on *process* or *product*?
9. In your building/district, how are educators put in *fight-or-flight* moments? Do you encourage and give the time to seek them out themselves, or are they pushed there?

Professionally Driven Educator
Jen Servais
High School Science Teacher &
Professional Development Coordinator

Jen plays many roles at Kee High in Lansing, IA. Not only does she go on her own Professionally Driven journeys as a science teacher, but she helps other educators with theirs as an instructional coach. In her own words, this is her first journey about how she wanted to infuse more growth mindset in her science classroom with her students.

There were a lot of contributing factors that brought Professionally Driven PD to our district. The frustrations that we felt in our district were not uncommon throughout the profession. Frustrations among teachers about PD topics that don't fit their needs or help them grow professionally and a desire from administrators to make PD more meaningful and applicable were two factors, but mostly it was a Teacher Leadership Grant that allowed the district to look at the direction of professional development and put someone in charge of making a change. That person ended up being me.

As I learned more about the Professionally Driven PD model, I loved the idea of giving PD back to the teachers. For many years, our district organized the whole group PD, and for years that approach was meaningful to only a handful of staff. It seemed like most topics didn't apply to certain content areas, and there was never enough time to explore topics in a way that allowed for meaningful implementation. My job was to coordinate this new method into the middle and high school. Although the coordination aspect was exciting and new, the more I learned about the model, the more excited I was to start my *own* Professionally Driven PD journey.

My first learning journey on the Professionally Driven model was to implement a growth mindset curriculum into my biology classroom. After attending a conference, I was struck by the idea that educators have not taught kids how to learn! For weeks, I couldn't stop thinking about this idea. Is it that obvious? In the race to cover content and test kids, did we forget the beginning step? Was this something that could be tested or proved? All these questions led me to identifying my weak spot and finding a topic that could have a positive impact on learner outcomes: *Can teaching growth mindset skills help with student achievement?*

The timing was perfect as we were implementing a new curriculum to all 9th and 10th graders. The ideas behind growth mindset were being presented to half of the high school's student body. The best part was knowing I would have all the time I needed to focus on this journey because time was already dedicated as part of our district plan for PD for the year. I knew I would have time available to me for the Research and Implementation phases of my plan *and,* for the first time in a long time, I was excited about professional development.

I started my journey in the Research phase by studying the work of Carol Dweck and Trevor Ragan. The premise is that we, as educators, need to teach kids how to learn in order for them to reach their educational potential. I spent the summer looking at growth mindset curriculum and decided to implement Growth Mindset Fridays for the first trimester of school. The data I used was derived from a self-assessment survey each student took to rate their growth mindset skills and knowledge. This was administered on the first day of school and the last day of the trimester. I also created a feedback survey for students to take at the end of the trimester. I struggled with the data piece as I wanted more quantitative data, but realized that qualitative data was just as useful and important.

The biggest obstacle I encountered was during the Integration phase in leading students to commit to the Growth Mindset Fridays routine by overcoming negative attitudes. There were several times I thought about skipping our Friday activities because we were behind in our biology activities, but I stayed the course and adjusted the classroom activities to make sure we kept a consistent and organized way to present the growth mindset information. The second obstacle involved one of the three classes not buying into the activities. They were openly hostile about the ideas behind growth mindset, and there were several times I thought about dropping the activities for that class. However, in the end, I decided I couldn't ask them to work on their perseverance if I was going to quit because they were being difficult.

As I worked through the Integration phase, I was simultaneously working on the Reflection phase. While I found parts of the Integration phase stressful or disappointing, there were great successes, too! The data collected indicated that 88% of students used growth mindset ideas at least once a week (outside of our classroom) and 98% of students improved on their growth mindset assessment score. Along with the growth of the students, I felt that the development of a growth mindset vocabulary was a huge success. Our shared vocabulary allowed us to refer back to the concepts throughout the year in a way that everyone understood.

As I continued to reflect, I found other ideas I wanted to put into action. I plan on rearranging the topics and incorporating more activities requiring students to converse about the topics at home. I will introduce the topics and vocabulary to all staff so the ideas are reinforced throughout the school. I am hoping to add Leadership Fridays to the second trimester as a way to teach some basic leadership skills (this might be my second Professionally Driven PD journey!)

One of the greatest aspects of the Professionally Driven model is the ability to have PD time during the work day where I could perfect my plan and bounce ideas and problems off my fellow staff members. This was crucial to the success of the plan. The collaboration that occurred during this time also led to staff members becoming invested in my idea and plan, leading them to stop and ask how things were going or sending relevant materials my way when they came across them. The level of collaboration skyrocketed.

The last two steps of Professionally Driven PD allowed me to present my journey to the staff in our building and share it outside of the district. The Sharing phase was important because doing so brought out new ideas and has led to several conversations with other staff members about how they can reinforce those same ideas in their own classroom. As I look forward to my next journey up the Professionally Driven mountain, I will continue to implement Growth Mindset Fridays in my classroom. In the end, the Professionally Driven model gave me the opportunity to explore a meaningful topic, increased collaboration with my colleagues, and brought enthusiasm to my professional growth.

CHAPTER 3
INTRINSIC MOTIVATION AND PROFESSIONAL DEVELOPMENT

We can't light for educators the fiery passion to learn, nor should we. But we can provide the right conditions and the flint.

In the previous chapter, I discussed my belief in my abilities to run a marathon, and I really do believe it is possible. What I lack, however, is the desire to do so. To me, running a marathon is not a goal of mine and nothing about it really ignites any fire within me. But you know what does motivate me to run? Mud. I love mud runs. By adding obstacles and mud, I have been motivated to train for and run a half marathon mud run. I've even scoped out full marathon mud run in hopes of completing one someday. You can even run a marathon and have colored powder thrown at you. You can run a marathon that includes inflatable obstacles. There are even distance running events where Zombies chase you (which is a whole other level of motivation.) It goes back to the old adage: *you can lead a horse to water, but you can't make him drink.* Maybe the horse wanted lemonade instead? The horse may *believe* in his ability to walk the great distance, but may be unwilling if he knows water is waiting for him. Do we put lemonade in the trough to motivate him? Or do we wait until he's thirsty enough to motivate himself?

The horse in this scenario is like some educators today. I often hear "reluctant" educators being labeled as fixed mindset if they are not willing to comply with the yearly initiative. *Non-compliance does not equal fixed mindset.* An educator could strongly believe in their ability to learn anything and have a growth mindset, but they may not be willing to comply because they don't think the yearly initiative is a good fit for their learners. This is where traditional professional development falls short. We need to create the learning environment for adults where they become thirsty to learn and drive their own learning.

Let's face it, traditional professional development isn't the most intrinsically motivating. Often times, it feels more like a *have-to-know* rather than a *want-to-know*, which I see as being the main difference between extrinsic and intrinsic motivation. In his book *Drive: The Surprising Truth About What Motivates Us* (2011), Daniel Pink lays out research that helps to demystify motivation. In some cases, it's a real eye-opener. Perhaps the most common sense fact in the book, however, is that intrinsic motivation is longer-lasting because of an internal drive, whereas extrinsic motivation is a shorter-lived external drive. Of course, if I am internally motivated to do something, there is a far greater chance that I will apply *perseverance* (or *grit*, according Angela Duckworth) when circumstances become difficult. When faced with that fight-or-flight situation, intrinsic motivation is what can aide in convincing me to go the route of *fight*.

So why do we not make every attempt possible to embed intrinsic motivation into our professional development if we know it to be far more effective in the long run? Answer: embedding extrinsic motivation is easier and more tangible. It's easier to think, *I need educators motivated now,* which is short-term thinking. This is why the motivational piece is usually tied to **training**, not **learning**.

TRAINING VS. LEARNING

Through my conversations with teachers, administrators, and coaches alike, it has become apparent that there is a mixture of conversations regarding what PD really is, and the language we use when referring to it is shaping the context around it. I do a great deal of listening in my role as a consultant. I listen for what people are saying about PD—how much time should be spent, who should deliver it, what is the teacher's role, how do we hold teachers accountable, and a slew of frustrations that go along with these kinds of subtopics. But when I listen more carefully to these conversations, I can begin to sort them into two major categories: *training* and *learning*. Let me visually sort out for you what I often hear, and I'll let you mentally add to either column based on your own experiences.

Training	Learning
What we **have to** know.	What we **want to** know.
Someone else determines the end goal.	**I** determine the end goal.
A linear method to complete a task.	**A process** that may not be linear in its completion.
Static	**Organic**
Often delivered **top-down**.	Often ignited from the **bottom-up**.
Often feels "**force-fed**"	Learner feels "**hungry**" to know.
Usually meant for **whole school** initiatives.	Usually meant for **individual** or **small groups**
Extrinsic motivators are attached for compliance.	Driven by **intrinsic motivation** because there is no need for compliance.
When learners don't comply and extrinsic motivators didn't work, **accountability** pieces are used to reinforce compliance.	Again, if learners aren't intrinsically motivated to learn, there is no need for **accountability**.
Developed for short-term understanding.	**Not developed**, it has existed for eons.

Again, this table is my interpretation of conversations over the last 11 years. I imagine that you have heard similar phrases that would fall into one of those two subcategories. At least, that is what my brain does when I hear administrators or teachers talk about PD. Essentially, I view my brain as operating like a factory assembly line. It receives bits of raw materials that first get sorted into *training* or *learning*. Then it moves into one of these other subcategories for further analysis. By sorting these PD conversations into the first two initial categories of *training* or *learning*, I am able to better facilitate further conversations around professional development. It's not uncommon for me to pose the question, "Are we talking about training teachers or letting them learn?" I will often follow up this question with a small activity with administrators where we audit the multitude of district initiatives that are being stoked in the fire. We literally sort each initiative into either a *training* column or *learning* column: "Is this a *want* to know or a *have* to know?" Once administrators realize that most, if not all, fall under *training*, they can see where time for *learning* has been pushed to the wayside. This is also when they begin to understand why, possibly, teachers are feeling frustrated with PD and are reluctant to participate in a meaningful way.

I'm not sure when, but at some point professional development became primarily training, and districts began to expect educators to do learning on their own time. And if they chose not to (probably because they are trying to deal with all of the responsibilities that come along with teaching, as well as the training that has been bestowed upon them), they are quickly labeled as a "lazy" educator. I said this in the previous chapter, but I feel it's worth mentioning again here: *forcing teachers to learn on their own time should **not** be some kind of test to determine the "motivated" teachers from the "lazy" ones.* This is no different than using the idea of homework in the same fashion and then giving kids the same labels.

However, in my conversations with leadership teams (these usually include administrators, coaches, and sometimes teachers), I will often hear, "But if the teacher is learning something new in the training that they didn't know before, isn't that learning?" Technically, yes. I never said there is no time for training or that training should be cut altogether. I'm merely advocating for a balance. In fact, I would argue that in the process of learning, training may be necessary.

If I am wishing to shift my classroom to a more blended learning environment, and in the process of researching more about it I find out I need to use a learning management system, I may need to seek out some training on a specific learning management system. This allows me to build the basic knowledge required to help me successfully implement the larger idea of blended learning. The training should be treated as something smaller and embedded within the learning process. It should not be a focal point for extrinsic motivators to be attached; instead, it should be naturally embedded in an intrinsically motivating process.

REWARDING COMPLIANCE VS. RECOGNIZING LEARNING

I don't need to go into great depth about the effects that rewards can have on motivation; Pink's book does that thoroughly enough for all of us, clearly pointing out to us the short-term effects that go along with them. Instead, I will discuss *how* rewards have been used in education and what effects I have personally observed.

There is a growing trend that I see being presented at conferences called *gamification*. This is the idea that gaming techniques can be applied to the process of learning in order to make it more fun for the participants. Jane McGonigal (@avantgame) is perhaps the leading figure in the concept of gamification. She has published two books and delivered a TED Talk on the matter. She speaks about the positive effects gaming can have on the brain, such as the release of certain chemicals that produce feelings of happiness. She provides some points that are hard to argue, and it's not my intent to do so.

Where it becomes grey, however, is when we consider the idea of rewarding for completing certain levels or attaining certain skills, and what we know about the use of rewards when it comes to intrinsic motivation. I don't argue that the use of rewards isn't helpful within the game in order to drive a player to reach the next level, but what about when the game is completed? I was one of those gamers that applied my Type A personality to each game. I would become obsessed with not just beating the game, but going back through as many times as were necessary in order to unlock other worlds and complete all of them. In terms of the glass half-full or half-empty analogy, I was one that wanted to complete or collect *everything* in the game in order to feel that the glass was completely full. But what happens at this point? For me, and I know the same is true for many gamers, the game gets stashed somewhere and collects dust. It's complete, it's done, and I'm ready to shell out more money for the next game. This leads an industry to keep cranking out more games that apply the same rewarding techniques, which is a great business model. This sounds a lot like how some students have played the game of school: do everything they need to do to get that A, call it good, and move on.

Where gaming becomes a powerful tool is where players must use problem-solving skills to move farther in the game. This is where the intrinsic motivation takes place. I have to use upper-level thinking (mainly Analyzing and Evaluating) in order to complete the tasks laid out before me in the game. But that's the problem: *tasks laid out for me*. I see this as being the key difference in *Rewarding vs. Recognizing* and how it applies to motivation.

Rewarding implies that a bar or tasks were set for me and I must work to complete them, much like the rewarding system used in gaming. Now, the concept of badging is beginning to build steam in education. In my opinion, badging is a rewards-system focused on extrinsic motivation disguised as an intrinsic motivator. In order to explain what I mean by this, let's first consider the purpose of badging.

Intrinsic motivation really occurs when we are able to share something and be recognized positively for our work/ accomplishments. We are then more inclined to continue that work in the long term. Badging attempts to do this by providing something representative of my work that I can share and be recognized for. But the operative word in that last sentence is *work*. Who is assigning the work to be done? This is the determiner for whether it is extrinsic or intrinsic motivation.

For example, with the idea of gaming, once I have accomplished a goal that was set before me by the developers, I may receive a badge that I can share with other gamers. I may be recognized positively by my peers, but because the tasks were laid out for me by the developers, the badge acts more as a carrot. The positive recognition that I receive from my peers, in this case, then intrinsically motivates me to attain more carrots. Put another way, *it intrinsically motivates me to attain more extrinsic motivators based on tasks determined by someone else*. This is how I see badging being used in most cases and also presented at most conferences. Some may argue that certifications work similarly to badging, as *it is a thing that I can show others*. But how was that certificate attained? Who determined the work that needed to be done to attain the certification? If the answer is someone else, I would argue that badging and certifications act more as rewards.

I want to shift the mindset in regards to motivation and professional development *to move completely away from anything that may resemble extrinsic motivation*. That means that when we are looking to design professional development models, we have to go back to the very start and establish two rules:

1. **The educator** must be the one to determine the learning journey, not someone else, and the journey can't simply be chosen from a "list" that is predetermined by someone else. This gives the illusion of choice and thwarts intrinsic motivation.
2. The journey, in its entirety, can't simply be **training** (as we have defined in the chart presented earlier in the chapter).

That means, from the very start, intrinsic motivation is initiated and sustained through the whole journey. That should be the goal of any professional development model because we know from studies cited in Daniel Pink's book that it is far more long-term and meaningful. These two rules also show an attempt to focus back on a holistic professional development process of *learning*, not training.

So if the initial goal of identifying an instructional weakness and turning it into a strength (as laid out in the previous chapter) is determined by the educator, that means the steps in that process are also determined by the educator. Therefore, the idea of *rewarding* can't even be applied, because neither the initial goal nor the process to achieve that goal is determined by someone else. However, in order for us to maintain the intrinsic motivation through the whole process of learning, we must include pieces to *recognize* educators at the varying stages of their learning journey.

It's similar to mountain climbing. There are camps established at various altitudes that help determine which stage of the journey climbers are on. On larger mountains, it is very difficult—practically impossible—to scale the whole mountain in a single trip. In most cases, climbers break at these camps to take inventory, look over the maps, analyze weather conditions, and talk with their climbing team before venturing onto the next leg of their journey. While that camp may indicate which stage of the journey they are on, how they got to that camp *was completely determined by them*. I see the process of learning much like mountain climbing. It's important for educators to be able to determine where to start their journey and be able to recognize where they are in that journey. Using **recognition pieces** help signify the whole process, not just *reward* the finished product.

If we are to apply the same mountain climbing metaphor to training, training would be what takes place prior to the climbing venture. It's the prerequisite knowledge attained, or the "what I need to know" before setting forth. However, if we only recognize the training portion with a badge or certification, then we are only recognizing a very small portion of the journey. As I said before, training is sometimes necessary in a learning journey, but it's not the whole journey. We also can't simply say to educators, "Here's the badge for completing the training (whether I determined the need for the training or you did), now go do something with it." This leaves them high and dry. It puts too much emphasis on the training and not nearly enough on the larger learning journey that should follow.

This idea of focusing on the whole journey and not just a single part of it has been around for thousands of years. Usually we find this idea emphasized in epic stories from as far back as *The Odyssey* to modern day *Star Wars*. Each protagonist embarking on their journey could not have come to the final change in beliefs without experiencing the whole journey, not just a small part of it.

THE HERO'S JOURNEY & PROFESSIONAL DEVELOPMENT

As an English teacher, I have used novels such as *Huck Finn* and *The Odyssey* in my classroom. Both are classic stories of epic journeys. More modern novels of popularity such as *Harry Potter* and *The Hunger Games* could be included in this category. While my students at the time may not have preferred *The Odyssey*, they certainly gravitated towards these more modern novels that continue to depict the kind of holistic journey that their predecessors did. These protagonists are often labeled as the hero of the story, and while the exact details from their journey differ from one story to the next, there have been commonalities that continue to resonate so strongly with the human spirit.

The idea of the Hero's Journey was first proposed by Joseph Campbell in *The Hero with a Thousand Faces* (1949). In this book, Campbell does a complete narrative analysis of dozens of stories that span the course of time, including myths and other fictional narratives. In doing so, he spells out what he believes to be the 12 phases that most narrative heroes go through in the completion of their journey. These elements can also be found in most journeys we embark on, and the connection between the Hero's Journey and the Professionally Driven journey is uncanny.

1. STATUS QUO

Where the journey takes place, the setting for our hero. In the educator's profession, this would simply be the school district, the building, or even the classroom.

2. CALL TO ADVENTURE

The hero is summoned to set forth. Once an educator identifies a weakness (as mentioned in the previous chapter), they now have the direction in which to go forth on their learning journey. However, the path is not laid out for them or predetermined. No one is standing at the beginning, pointing and saying, "Go that way." The educator is the one empowered to do this.

3. ASSISTANCE

The hero gets help from someone else when they become stuck on their journey. This is where Yoda played a role in the movie *Star Wars.* On any journey worth taking, the learner will feel stuck from time to time. In the case of an educator, this assistance can come from another educator (teacher or administrator), instructional coach, or even another colleague that they have connected with on Twitter or any other social media used for their professional learning network (PLN). Having these people in place prior to starting the journey can help tremendously.

4. DEPARTURE

The hero leaves the safety of their *Ordinary World* and ventures to the *Special World*. What would the Ordinary World or Special World look like for educators? The easiest way to apply this would be in a metaphorical sense.

The Ordinary World would represent what the teacher finds to be comfortable. That could include **pedagogy** (teaching strategies, management strategies, etc.), **content** (how familiar a teacher is with their content, materials used to support their content, etc.), or even **technology use** (how comfortable an educator is in using a specific technology or technologies). These three areas are what is known as the TPaCK Framework, developed Mirsha and Koelher (2005) piggybacking off of the original PCK (Pedagogical Content Knowledge) framework from Lee Shulman (1986). Essentially, the Ordinary World would be looking at these areas and determining where an educator's comfortability level is with each.

In contrast, the Special World would be any area where an educator feels uncomfortable. If an educator identifies a particular weakness that may fall in the area of *pedagogy*, like Flipped Learning, for example, they now cross the metaphorical river over into that unknown world and begin exploring. In a nutshell: Ordinary World = areas of comfortability, Special World = areas of uncomfortability.

5. TRIALS

These are the moments of struggle and conflict that a hero endures on their journey. For the educator, it is the trial and error process that goes along with attempting anything new. There will be moments when you feel it just didn't work or you failed. But as you may recall from the previous chapter, this is where we build grit and perseverance. It's easier to choose *Fight* over *Flight* when you know that trial and error is just part of the larger journey that you are intrinsically motivated to finish.

6. APPROACH

The approach is the buildup to the ultimate conflict.

Stay with me on this one, but in the learning journey of an educator, the ultimate conflict to conquer is *fear*. Deep, I know, but it's true. In the example of Flipped Learning, for some teachers, allowing students to take control of the front loading of information is scary. I often hear teachers say, "If students are doing the lower-level front loading of information outside of my class, then what do we do INSIDE my class time?" When I hear this, I hear a fight-or-flight moment, because they have approached the scary monster that has triggered it.

7. CRISIS

The hero chooses to fight, may seem defeated, but comes back renewed and ready to attack. Continuing with the example of Flipped Learning, when I see a teacher come to that moment of fight-or-flight, I urge that teacher to stay in that moment of uncomfortability and fight through it. I try to be Yoda, asking questions to prompt more thinking. The only way for an educator to fight through those moments of uncomfortability is to *think through them*, or for some, *talk through them*.

Like students, educators also have a-ha moments. An a-ha moment is literally when two synapses connect in the brain and high dosages of positive hormones are released, one being dopamine. Therefore, the educator must be the one to think through those moments of uncomfortability. If I did it for them (which is what most traditional forms of training do), then I am literally robbing the educator of the ability to connect synapses. If I let them have their a-ha moment, dopamine will be released, and they will feel energized and motivated to continue tackling their fear.

8. TREASURE

The hero receives something in return for conquering the major conflict. This one is tricky, simply because I'm sure a lot of people will interpret it as receiving an award for performing a task. I think I've established in this chapter that the idea of awarding/rewarding is not the purpose of a journey. Therefore, if we continue to use The Hero's Journey as a metaphor, the treasure for conquering a fear will be *a greater sense of self*. Once again, not trying to be over-the-top philosophical, but it's true. I'm sure we have all experienced small moments where we have overcome a fear. What's the feeling that follows? A greater sense of self and a new sense of empowerment. This should be the treasure we seek, not a badge, certification, or reward of some kind.

9. RESULT

What happens as an outcome of receiving the treasure? Is our hero chased out of the Special World after conquering the beast? In some stories, yes. But in the case of a learning journey, once an educator conquers his or her fear and experiences a new sense of self, what are the next steps they take? In the Flipped Learning example, if the educator discovers that they need to strengthen their in-class activities to activate more upper-level thinking for students, the result may be a desire to further learn such strategies. However, the **result** can vary drastically from journey to journey. This is why it is ongoing.

10. RETURN

The hero, at last, must return to the Ordinary World. Of course, the educator isn't physically returning anywhere; they've been in the district/building/classroom the whole time. In this case, returning from the Special World to the Ordinary World means *the uncomfortable now feels comfortable.* I'm not returning to the beginning phase, as I once was. It means my Flipped Learning journey now feels complete because it feels comfortable to me and my students. Remember: Ordinary World = areas of comfortability; Special World = areas of uncomfortability.

11. NEW LIFE

The hero feels "changed" in some way. For educators, this goes back to Guskey's work, referenced in the previous chapter. The last phase in his model for professional development is *Change in Teacher Beliefs.* When an educator goes on a learning journey, they will experience this change in teaching beliefs. Through the power of reflection, educators can see and acknowledge this change.

12. RESOLUTION

There are often loose ends that must be tied up. Like any story, the hero's journey must have a resolution. In a learning journey, this could be a variety of things. It is completely dependent on the journey that was taken.

FROM A HERO'S JOURNEY TO A PROFESSIONALLY DRIVEN JOURNEY

Completing any journey similar to a Hero's Journey can be arduous, but it will be highly rewarding in the end. If professional development were treated as an opportunity for educators to go on their own hero's journey, perhaps they would find it to be just as rewarding.

So, if we were to apply this same concept to professional development, we would need to determine what the phases are of that Professionally Driven learning journey. I propose these four phases: **Research, Integrate, Reflect,** and **Share**.

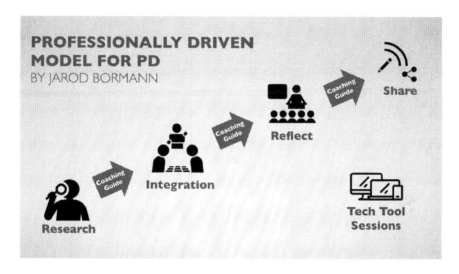

PHASE 1: RESEARCH

Researching is always a critical step when trying to gain new information on a topic. Educators are by nature very good researchers. We go to workshops and conferences, search for blogs, attend Edcamps, and reach out to other educators when we need more information about our content or profession. We are informally researching all the time. *Any of these examples would count as research in this particular phase.* Research does not have to mean seeking out peer-reviewed journal articles. Researching is simply seeking out, from *any* resource, new information. However, in this Professionally Driven model, research is done with the intent to actually put it to work.

Going out and finding information is never the problem for educators. In a lot of cases, it's usually the **topic** that causes the most trouble. Most educators catch wind of a new classroom trend and go find more information, but this can be dangerous. That's right, I said *dangerous.* How do you know this trend is good for your students? I work with some educators that are the "trendsetters" in their district, always trying to stay abreast with the latest buzzwords that float around Twitter. I'm not saying that using Twitter to research and gain new knowledge is a bad thing; I am a huge proponent of it. But I do not endorse trying on the latest buzzwords like articles of clothing at the mall to see if they make you look cooler. While you're looking at yourself in the mirror, your students are standing off to the side saying, "*Really?!*"

It's the difference between *buying* and *shopping*. If an educator identifies their weakness first, they will research with a purpose. That's *buying*, just like a customer who first identifies what it is they need before they go out to find it. When we go to Amazon, we usually have in mind what we want to get before booting up the computer or opening the app. An educator who *shops*, on the other hand, is one who might go to an Edcamp or conference just to see what conversations are happening. This isn't a bad thing, but just like an impulse shopper, you may end up taking something home that you (or your students) may not have truly needed in the first place.

Have purpose for your research and your learning. It's seeing the top of the mountain and working to understand the best route to get there. If a teacher just attends conferences and Edcamps without actually having a vision for what they'd like to improve in their classroom, then all they're doing is walking around the base of the mountain, trying various paths with no intent of actually reaching the summit. Simply researching and learning new tech tools or a new trend here or there is not the summit...not even close. Professionally Driven educators see the summit and are willing to put in the work to get there. In this case, the summit is the positive effects on learner outcomes.

PHASE 2: INTEGRATE
Integration is the phase that is often left out of other professional development models. Once educators have self-identified a weakness in their instruction (Chp. 2), teachers can be given all the time in the world to go research, but it doesn't do any good unless they are also given time to **integrate** that research into their classroom. They need to be given the time and support for trial-and-error. It's through this process that teachers will further develop their growth mindset and at the same time, hone the instructional strategy that they researched. Once they know what path to take up the mountain, they need to be given the time and support to begin the journey upward.

There are several important questions for an educator to consider during this phase:

- What steps need to be taken?
- What resources or technologies need to be pulled in to integrate your research?
- What worked? What didn't work?
- What changes have you seen with how you teach?
- What changes have you seen in how your students are learning?
- What will you look for to know if it's working or not?

The last question is the most important. Educators need to be thinking about how they will determine if the strategy is working or not. This formative data could be whatever it needs to be so long as it relates to the topic identified by the teacher. This could be:

- formative assessment results
- summative assessment results
- a poll administered to the students
- a survey
- informal conversations with students
- any other indicators of success with integration

Since teachers will most likely be spending class time integrating their new strategy, it would be in their best interest to use personalized PD time to reflect on this formative data and determine if retooling is necessary to achieve better results (use of time in this manner explained further in Chapter 5). This process of trial-and-error could be a fairly lengthy one, depending on the strategy the teacher is looking to implement. If the teacher is attempting to work towards a flipped learning environment, they could be spending months, or even a year or two, in the Integration phase of this personalized PD model. *This is absolutely OK and encouraged.* A Professionally Driven journey is about quality, not quantity. An educator's Professionally Driven journey will hardly ever begin at the start of the school year, nor will it end at the conclusion of the school year. Learning is an ongoing process and should be treated as such.

PHASE 3: REFLECT

The main objective of the Reflection phase is to simply **share** your Professionally Driven journey with your fellow colleagues within your district. Think of it as a *Show and Tell* for educators. However, through this process of sharing, the intent is for the educator to reflect on the *journey* that they have completed, not necessarily the *final product*.

How exactly the educator shares out to their colleagues is completely up to them. One format that I like to use is 10-minute TED-style talks. This gives the educator the proper setting to tell their story. Too many times, when there is something good happening in the classroom, teachers only tell one another in the teacher's lounge. However, conversations can quickly turn negative when the topic of unruly students is brought up. A TED-style talk is perfect for having the proper attention to reflect back on your Professionally Driven journey and share your story with your peers.

I know that some educators have anxiety at the idea of speaking in front of their colleagues. That is why I encourage any method of sharing out, *so long as it is done within the district.* Some teachers may opt to simply make a video that includes footage from the classroom as well as themselves speaking to the camera. This video can then be shared with the entire district as a large group or through email.

Other methods are welcome, but certain questions should be addressed in the reflection, including:

- What was the question/topic you were looking to tackle and *why*? (What was the weakness you were looking to turn into a strength?)
- What positive change in student outcomes were you hoping to achieve?
- What steps did you take?
- What worked/didn't work?
- What were moments of personal enlightenment (change in teacher beliefs?)
- What state teaching standards did you meet in the process?

Up to this point, we have not asked the teachers to focus on state teaching standards. We want the majority of the focus to be on their instruction and their efforts to make it better. In that process, they will naturally meet whatever state teaching standards are mandated, and it is at this point that we ask them to make those connections.

It's the Reflection phase that I feel is the most important in building true *intrinsic motivation*. Think about it. How do we motivate a reluctant learner in our classrooms? Most often, it's a matter of simply acknowledging their thoughts, ideas, and efforts and making them feel valued. That is exactly what we are trying to do in the Reflection phase; an educator shares their efforts in bettering their instruction, and that effort is being acknowledged by their colleagues in a positive way. This will hopefully intrinsically motivate the educator to continue that same process over and over again. What's being acknowledged is not simply the end result the educator achieved, but rather, the trials and errors that they overcame in order to gain that positive effect on learner outcomes. This also promotes a growth mindset in the teaching culture of your school.

I have personally seen learning fires become ignited as soon as the first reflection takes place. Those reflection talks generate an excitement that spreads like wildfire because others see that they also have permission to try integrating new instructional strategies. Educators become empowered when they see and hear that they have permission to make mistakes, just like kids, because making mistakes is *learning*. An emphasis on not making mistakes is *compliance*.

PHASE 4: SHARE

It may seem redundant to label this phase "Sharing" since educators already shared inside their district in the Reflection phase. However, educators shouldn't stop the sharing there. The ultimate goal and pinnacle of the learning journey is to encourage educators to share their new understanding/story *outside* their district. This can be done a number of ways:

- Blogging about your journey and sharing it via social media.
- Creating a video and uploading it to YouTube (and preferably sharing via other social media platforms as well).
- Presenting at a conference.

- Attending an Edcamp and lead a session on the topic.
- Joining a Voxer group related to your topic of learning and share your expertise.
- Any other method that promotes sharing your learning journey *outside* the district.

The ultimate goal in this phase is to promote educators to share their new ideas and connect with other like-minded educators. When others outside the district acknowledge the teacher's work and ideas, it only strengthens their intrinsic motivation to continue the natural learning process more times over. We know that educators hone their craft in more positive ways when they connect to the global education community. And when they do, they realize this natural learning process exists everywhere. Not only that, it is positive marketing for your school. If every educator in your district is sharing the great stuff happening inside your district to others outside the district, it creates a positive image for your school.

I have led whole-group professional development for educators about social media and how to use it to build a professional learning network. What inevitably happens is the educators that are already utilizing social media only continue to do so while the others (who did not even have an account) get set up with one that they will hardly ever use again. This is usually due to the fact that they don't have a context in which to use the social media. In this Sharing phase, they will have something worthy of sharing via social media, which means that they are more inclined to use it for what it is intended for. When educators see the need for it, we can also provide the 1-on-1 or small group time to learn the new tools, too.

TECH SESSIONS

In this Professionally Driven model, I wanted to make technology the lowest common denominator in the equation, emphasizing that it is a small part of the overall learning process. We don't want educators to start with the technology; we want them to start with the *pedagogy*. By focusing on the pedagogy, educators give a purpose to the use of technology. Teachers often ask me, "What new tools do you know?" My reply back to them is, "Well, what new teaching strategies are you trying to incorporate?" The tool should match the instructional strategy, not vice versa.

However, we do not eliminate technology or technology training altogether. Instead, we make it available when educators discover they need it. Since changing my role to a Technology Integration Specialist, I often hear from administrators, "Teachers don't know what they don't know." And while this may be true, who are we to pass down knowledge in a manner that may not be timely for teachers' needs? Instead, we want all educators to discover for themselves what it is they may not know and then seek out those experts that do know.

Tech Sessions are not predetermined by a technology coordinator or an administrator. Rather, Tech Session requests come from the educators. As an educator who is working in the Research phase or even the Integration phase, if you discover that you need something, then request it. If I'm a teacher who discovers in the Research phase of my flipped learning journey that I need to use a learning management system (LMS) to house all of my online materials, but I have no idea what that is, I just self-discovered what it is that I don't know and can now send in that request for a Tech Session.

I always recommend to schools that a designated person within the building or district be in charge of Tech Session requests. When an educator wishes to learn more about a particular tool, they email this designated person with a request. The Tech Session request person then decides one of four things:

1. Is this a request that only a particular educator is asking for that I may be able to help them with individually?
2. If more than one educator is requesting this tool, does this qualify as a tech session on our next personalized PD day?
3. As the Tech Session request person, if I don't feel comfortable with this tool, is there another educator in the building that I could reach out to in order to have them fulfill the request?
4. If this request is something that no one in our building or district is comfortable with, do I need to bring in outside support?

As you can see, the Tech Session request person may not necessarily be fulfilling the request but can vet the requests to the appropriate experts. However, in order to keep all lines of communication as clear as possible, I highly recommend all Tech Session requests go to *one* person. This will avoid email and communication confusion.

Tech Sessions do not need to be long. If a handful of educators are interested in a particular tool and are able to cover the tool with an expert in 20 minutes or so, they can use the rest of their personalized PD time to continue planning and playing with the tool. Once again, the educators are getting the tools that they identify they need when they need them and in the amount of time that they need them.

In order to maximize the allotted time, I would highly recommend that the Tech Session be held in the same designated area every time. That way, if an email the day before goes out reviewing the next Tech Session topic, everyone on staff knows where that session will be held. If it moves from room to room every month, it could become confusing for educators and take up precious learning time.

DRIVE THE WHOLE JOURNEY

These four main phases, along with embedding the idea of training (Tech Sessions), is a holistic process of learning for educators based on Guskey's model of professional development. No phase can be excluded or simply glazed over. Each one takes priority in order to complete the full journey. If you leave any phase out, you lose the full effect the journey can have on our change in teaching beliefs. It's a process that we can recognize and honor rather than *reward*. It's these four phases that allow for intrinsic motivation to fully drive the process from start to finish. By creating a process based on intrinsic motivation, we begin to address what I believe is the third major piece to a successful personalized professional development model that empowers educators to be Professionally Driven: sustainable autonomy.

QUESTIONS TO CONSIDER FOR MOTIVATION AND PROFESSIONAL DEVELOPMENT

Before moving on to the next chapter, I encourage you to reflect on these questions regarding intrinsic motivation and the current professional development in your district:

1. Are teachers allowed to determine their own learning paths in order to trigger intrinsic motivation? Allowing educators to only choose from a predetermined list is *not* the same.
2. If you were to make two columns on a piece of paper—one *Training* and the other *Learning*—based on what was discussed in this chapter, how much of your current PD would fall under each column?
3. Does your district use extrinsic motivators that emphasize a finished product, or do they use intrinsic motivators that emphasize and recognize a process?
4. What elements of the four phases purposed do you already have in place? Which phases would need to be included?

PROFESSIONALLY DRIVEN EDUCATOR
MARY BETH STEGGALL
Middle School Principal

It wasn't easy for Mary Beth to define her first journey right away at Oelwein, but it took listening and having several conversations with staff members for her to discover where the weakness was. Listen to her journey in her own words as she pinpoints the lightbulb moments from an administrator's perspective.

The day that a special meeting was called for the Oelwein administration team to discuss a new model of PD for educators promoting personalized professional development and integrating technology into their classroom is a day that will always stand out to me. While listening to Jarod explain the Professionally Driven model, I was excited to see our focus shift from traditional PD to teachers choosing their own path of professional development. Each phase of the journey recognized teacher growth and when they completed that level of the journey they received a flag to honor their accomplishment. The flag was to be hung in their classroom with pride to display to staff and students their accomplishments.

I supported the Professionally Driven model 100%. What a great concept, teachers responsible for their own learning! As I sat and listened to the components of each phase, I remember all the questions that raced through my head. As a new middle school administrator, how was I going to be able to support our educators with my early childhood background? I had been a kindergarten teacher and a K-1 administrator. Struggling with the impossible task, I turned to humor that I would be the "cook" at base camp and teachers would be fed well as they prepared for their journey up the mountain. After a few days of joking, the realization of how to support all educators consumed me.

I believe that if an administrator is going to call themselves a lead learner, then they have to do just that. I am not the type of leader to stand and watch the educators in our building go through the journey alone, I wanted to go through the journey with them. In order to understand the needs of all of our educators going through the journey, I spent hours researching, talking to our superintendent, speaking with Jarod and our instructional coaches about how to best support our educators. They assured me that I would be able to support all educators and that they would also be there every step of the journey. I didn't feel prepared at the time and early on I often had more questions and concerns that I wouldn't be able to provide all the resources our educators needed to be successful.

Despite my fears, we embraced a growth mindset and began the Integration phase. As time went on and the Professionally Driven model was launched, I supported our educators by conferencing with them to discuss their progress, encouraging them, and honoring educators' time to work. We supported the process by ensuring all educators had time and opportunities to meet with the instructional coaches and Jarod to help answer questions and concerns that I could not. At this point I was more a guide on the side, cheering them on to keep going, but a pivotal moment in my own journey was about to take place.

On an early dismissal day, all educators were working on their Professionally Driven journeys, and I stopped in to visit with an educator to see how her journey was progressing. This conversation, as it turned out, was going to inspire me towards my own journey. While visiting with her she shared what she had been working on for her journey. After discussing this for some time, she shared a video that she wanted her students to view. This video, "One Day Kindness Boomerang," sparked an idea for me. I asked her if she would mind if I used the video with some of our students that struggled with positive behaviors. That weekend it came to me to create a class designed for these struggling students with the potential to change their lives! At this moment I started my own Professionally Driven journey: "Husky Acts of Kindness."

When I knew the path I wanted to embark on, I followed the same Professionally Driven model that I had challenged our educators with. The main goal was to help provide a positive experience for our students struggling with behavioral concerns, but the fact is I also needed and wanted to understand the process and the expectations that were set forth for our educators. When I began my journey, I felt overwhelmed and I had a better understanding of what our educators must be going through. I had never taught at the middle school level and the pieces to my project were fragmented. This was one of the many emotions that I felt when I started. Realizing a sense of confusion and lack of direction lead me to a long-needed conversation with Ms. [Jill] Kelly, the instructional coach, and a second transformational moment occurred. (See Jill's vignette later in the book.)

My Tech Session time with Ms. Kelly was the biggest *a-ha* moment of my journey. From the beginning I was focused on the wrong part of the journey: technology tools! I was concerned with the tools I would use to help students when instead I needed to focus on student outcomes. What do I want my students to learn and how will I know when they have achieved the goal? When I knew what mountain I wanted to climb—fostering positive student behaviors—I began heading forward. Along the way, I found we had many experts in our building, educators who were more than happy to point me in the right direction. If the educators in our building didn't know the answer, they had developed a PLN and were able to suggest another educator I could connect with. Soon after this Tech Session, the fragmented pieces started fitting together like a puzzle. Each piece building on the next, connecting my journey with broader goals such as 21st Century Skills, Common Core Standards and various school initiatives.

During my Professionally Driven journey, the students I worked with took ownership of the project and helped drive its direction. Students created a website, a blog, a Twitter account, and a Facebook page. Students felt pride in belonging to the group and designed a t-shirt for the group, locker tags, and a video. The group dynamic of the students I began this journey with completely changed! In the beginning, I spent countless days and hours focusing on changing behaviors, a positive outcome for students, and it worked! Now we spend our time working on *our* project, and I am thankful our students helped me grow as a professional.

Embarking on the Professionally Driven journey helped me to better understand and support the educators in our building and has changed me as an educator and principal. As I look to continue on my journey, I will continue to seek advice from others. In going through this process, I have a better understanding of the questions and frustrations educators go through. Sometimes you simply need to be there to listen while they are trying to figure out the next step. Like any journey, there are going to be days where the trail is level ground and easily traversed, and other days the trail is steep and the struggles are difficult. Whether teachers traveled the trail alone or with a colleague, reaching the summit always provides a great sense of pride! During the Reflection phase, the ability to share your journey with colleagues provides a great sense of accomplishment.

To this day, I still have the summit flag hanging in my office along with a note from a student who was with me every step on the climb. The student wrote to me at the end of the school year, "I finally feel a part of something. Thank you Mrs. Steggall." While I began the journey intending to provide a positive change for students, to change student outcomes and reinforce positive behaviors, I ended my first climb realizing how much the journey changed me and our school culture for the better!

CHAPTER 4
SUSTAINABLE AUTONOMY AND PROFESSIONAL DEVELOPMENT

It's not enough to merely incite educators to become intrinsically motivated, we must also create an environment that allows them do so.

Another major theme in professional development that has become very apparent in my short 11 years in education is the lack of sustainability. I'm not questioning whether education itself is sustainable, rather the teaching and assessment trends that seem to make their way into education, fade, and then come back relabeled as something else. I don't think I've been in education long enough to experience the recycling of trends, but I've seen some fade, and I've heard veteran educators say, "Well, we called that (X) some odd years ago, and it didn't work then!" This leads me to ask, "Did it really not work or was it just not treated as something that was meant to be sustainable in the first place?" If the answer is the latter, then I ask, "Was it just put in place to fix a perceived current 'problem' and never intended to be a long-term solution?"

We've often heard, "The problem with education is (X)." We've also heard a variety of categories that replace X, followed by a so-called solution. Let me ask you, in all the times we've heard this, how many have seemed long-term or sustainable? Current problems reflect what is happening now, not in the past or the future. Therefore, any solutions tend to focus on the same. So to prompt my own thinking, I asked myself, *What would sustainability in education look like?* However, before we attempt to answer that question, we should first try to answer, *What kills sustainability in education?*

SUSTAINABILITY KILLERS

The idea of sustainability in education is something that I literally lie awake at night contemplating. Why is it that we see very little that "sticks" while almost everything else falls to the wayside? When it comes to education, how do you prevent something with significance from falling off the radar? Though there are veteran educators out there with far more experience than myself, I have made some observations that didn't come to light until I changed positions from classroom teacher to area educational consultant. Therefore, the following observations should be treated as just that: observations. However, when I reach out to my Professional Learning Network (PLN) to see if they observe the same things that I do, it does seem to reaffirm that the following are recurring themes that are likely killing sustainability in education: 1) yearly initiatives, 2) accountability, and 3) a top-down mentality.

1. YEARLY INITIATIVES

As a classroom teacher, a routine was established where at the beginning of every school year, the staff would congregate in a central location and the administrative team would reveal that year's "initiative." I can recall many initiatives that were started but never completed with fidelity: differentiated instruction, formative assessments, rigor and relevance, and a variety of tech tool trainings that followed going 1:1 as a district. I'm sure you can easily recall initiatives you experienced that also came and quickly passed. Some of these spanned a couple of years but ultimately faded as the next yearly initiative came into light. In his book, *Transforming Professional Development into Student Results (2010)*, Douglas B. Reeves calls this **initiative fatigue**. I chalk up the idea of yearly initiatives as a sustainability killer for two reasons:

Yearly initiatives condition teachers to be passive when it comes to learning.

As I've mentioned before, I have heard teachers labeled as "lazy" because they don't carry out the initiative with fidelity in their classroom. But a teacher can easily develop the mindset, "All I have to do is fake it 'til I make it, because there will be another initiative next year." I have heard those exact words directly from the mouths of more than one educator. In fact, I will admit that I began to develop the same mindset as a classroom teacher. Why? Because in most cases, the initiative is top-down. It's a "have to" and not a "want to." Therefore, it is treated as a means of compliance, which takes us back to the previous chapter on motivation. Some may cast the blame on the teacher for developing this mindset, but I cast blame on the routine of yearly initiatives.

A lightbulb moment for me as a teacher was when I was passing back tests that we had taken over a particular novel. I was student-teaching at a high school in 2006, and you will likely chuckle when you realize my rookie mistake. As I passed them back, I handed one student his test who had received a "B," and as he noticed his score, he said out loud, "Sweet! I didn't even read the book!" Students laughed awkwardly, anticipating that I would begin chastising on how he should have put the work in and what he missed out on by not reading the book. I, however, was frozen and dumbfounded and wasn't sure how to react. I went home that night and reflected hard on *what I did to enable this*?

Each chapter, we had a set of discussion questions that we hashed out as a large group in class. We also had a review packet with all of the discussion questions in it. We reviewed in game-style for the test, which was primarily the discussion questions. Finally, I administered a test that was, for the most part, multiple choice, fill-in-the-blank, and short answer questions. When I reflected on the steps we had taken, I realized that I had given students every excuse *not* to read the book. I enabled that. Me, not anyone else.

Similarly, when we create an environment of professional development that enables educators to develop passive mindsets, who should we blame? The ones that participate in that environment or the creators? Notice I did not say *teachers* or *administrators*. I do not like pointing blame, because that gets us nowhere. But when it comes to traditional PD, there are the creators (whomever that should be) and the participators (whomever that should be). To assume that teachers fall in one group and administrators fall in the other would be naive, because that may not be the case for all schools.

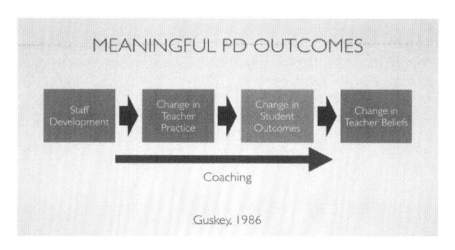

73

Yearly initiatives do not close the gap between *Staff Development* **and** *Change in Teacher Practice.*

Reference back to Guskey's model (1986) for Meaningful PD Outcomes above. In his chart, each phase is equally spaced, but in reality, there is a massive chasm between these first two phases with nothing more than a feeble rope bridge connecting them. We've seen those moments in movies: a dilapidated rope bridge that seems ancient and a mile long with someone on the other side yelling, "Come on, you got this!" The person crosses gingerly and hesitantly as each small gust of wind rocks the bridge and stirs up the fear once again, eventually leaving them frozen in the middle.

In traditional forms of PD that go along with yearly initiatives, educators receive the staff development but are just "expected" to then perform the next phase, *Change in Teacher Practice*. In most cases, little support is given in that phase. However, more and more schools, like the ones I work with in Iowa, are creating instructional coaching positions within their district in order to provide that in-house support when educators need it. Guskey showed us that this role is crucial, and we are now seeing the gains from it. These roles are also being added across the nation and new hashtags are popping up on Twitter that relate to instructional coaching. The works of Jim Knight and Diane Sweeney are becoming the go-to trainings for such a position, but an important thing to remember is crossing the chasm from *Staff Development* to *Change in Teacher Practice* takes **time**. Some may take the challenge head-on and cross that rope bridge more quickly while others may be more hesitant.

Is their hesitation simply "unwillingness," or is it due to a lack of buy-in from the start because the PD creators have laid the path for them, not the participants themselves? Therefore, if PD creators move on to the next initiative before the participant has had time to even cross the first chasm, they are less likely to be willing to attempt to cross it again, because they weren't given enough time to even cross the first one. Repeat this over the course of years, and you will quickly see why educators can become "cynical," "lazy," or "reluctant." But if you ask, *What about the educators that tackle the initiative head on and cross that chasm more quickly?* My reply would be, "Are those educators truly 'driven' or are they highly compliant?" I've heard educators say, "Just tell me what I need to do, and I'll get it done." This doesn't sound like a go-getter to me. This sounds like someone who has been very well-conditioned in the model of compliance, and in that model, there is very little room for active thinking.

- *Tell me what to do, and I'll do it.*
- *Am I doing it correctly?*
- *Is this right?*
- *What else do I need to do?*

All of these phrases imply, *Do the thinking for me, and I'll perform the dutiful action.* These are phrases I've heard from educators and even the top "A" students in my own classroom. Again, this is a mindset that we are conditioned into because someone else continuously lays out the path for us. We are also conditioned to fear diverging from that path. That's why we continuously ask if we are doing it correctly, and often hesitate to move forward if we hit a fork in the road. We're waiting for permission or confirmation to move forward in one direction or the other. In no way, shape, or form are we being cognitively operational in our own thinking, decision-making, or even actions.

Most yearly initiatives don't allot the proper time and support to allow for meaningful adoption of instructional change, nor are participants' input included in that initiative. Often times the PD creators are the ones to lay out the path for the PD participants, and to encourage them to "participate," the creators include "accountability."

2. *"ACCOUNTABILITY"*

Mention of the word **accountability** has become somewhat of a red flag for me when speaking with a district. In most cases, the word is used and associated with a model of compliance. Usually the initiative is a "have-to," and the idea of accountability is used to answer the question, "What about those that don't comply?" I alluded to this in my *Training vs. Learning* chart in the previous chapter on intrinsic motivation. That's because accountability is often used when incentives fail. *If the carrot didn't work, then we'll have to try the stick.* Again, if you read Daniel Pink's book, you'll understand the fallacy of such thinking.

The word has also developed a lot of negative connotations with educators, another reason why I dislike using the word in any kind of professional development model. If you don't believe that the word implies a business-as-usual mindset, then use it in front of a group of educators and watch the eye-rolls and invisible walls go up. Not only was I one of those educators, I've been in staff meetings and professional developments where the word was spoken out loud. You could almost hear the room become a construction zone as invisible fortresses of mistrust are erected with every sigh. It's discouraging to say the least. Accountability implies a lack of trust, and any kind of autonomy cannot exist in such an environment.

To be blunt, if you are working towards an environment where every educator is autonomous, and that autonomy is sustained because they are intrinsically motivated to seek out mastery, *then you shouldn't need accountability*. The word *accountability* should never be needed when discussing and purposefully planning professional development that is truly embedded on the idea of *learning*, not *training*. Just like yearly initiatives, accountability can lead to a conditioned mindset of compliance.

I was at a school district that was just starting off on their journey of implementing my Professionally Driven model. We had gone through the preliminary discussions, and educators were in the first couple of weeks of the model. On this particular day, educators had two hours of contractual professional development time to work on their Professionally Driven journeys. I was checking in with educators to see how things were going. I walked up to one educator who was the reading specialist in the elementary. "Hey, how's it going?" I said to break the ice, because she looked a little disgruntled about something.

"Fine," she replied, "but I'm not sure what you want me to do with my resources?"

"Resources from what?" I asked.

"I went to this training on the Wilson Reading System, and I'm not sure what you want me to do with the packets and resources that I got from it. Do I have to scan all these and put them in that Google Folder that we have set up for our personalized PD?" It was a valid question, but the tone she was using seemed to be indignant and getting to a question of compliance.

Calmly I said to her, "Well, scanning all this would seem silly. Tell me about the training? What were your biggest takeaways? Or maybe start with how you decided on this particular training for your first Professionally Driven journey?" She proceeded to give me the timeline and thinking that went behind how she got to that point. She even said that she has begun to implement it, and she is seeing great results.

"Do you have any numbers on that?" I asked. She navigated to a Google Sheet in her drive and began to excitedly explain the results that she had seen in just a month of implementing the program.

Excited for her, I said, "This all looks great. In fact, it sounds like you're ready for the Reflection phase."

She looked confused. "OK...but...what do I need to put into these Google Folders?"

Somewhat confused I replied, "Well, I would put that spreadsheet with the results in your Integration folder so others can see it if they wish to implement the same program."

"What about my Research folder? What do I *have* to have in there?" Her voice went back to a stand-offish tone, and I could tell what she was really trying to get to: *Tell me what it is I* **have** *to do in order to prove I did it?* Or to put it another way, *Where's the accountability piece?*

I replied, "Nothing if it's all in these booklets. This is a process of autonomous learning. There's no accountability piece here. All we ask is if you think you're ready for the next phase, then just sit down and have a conversation with one of your coaches, so we can ask you about the learning and see how we can continue to support you in this process, like what we just did. The folders are there if you need them. But if you put stuff in there from each phase, then it'll help some of your colleagues if they choose to go on a similar learning journey. There's no *have-to* in any of this. We just want to have conversations with you about your learning. That's all."

She didn't reply right away, but instead kind of looked at her resources for a few seconds in a way that almost made me feel I said something wrong, but I realized she was just trying to make sense of what I said. No one had ever told her that before.

She spoke while still staring at her materials, "There's always been something that I've had to do to prove I did it, and you're just telling me that all I have to do is talk with a coach?"

With a slight smile I said, "Well, we won't force you, but we'd really like you to so we can support you if necessary. We'd also like to be able to recognize you at the Recognition Ceremonies as you progress to each phase. If not, then we'll just stay out of your way. But learning what you're doing could help coaches support other educators, too." Another pause.

With a tone implying a weight had been lifted, "This is what it's supposed to be like. I feel like I've wasted 25 years of PD. This is what PD should be." Hearing such a statement from her, a 25-year veteran educator who I would label as professionally driven, validated what I had felt and known PD could be. She was an educator who had been conditioned to think of the accountability piece in any kind of new learning that she chose to embark on. If I want her to truly feel autonomous, I can't have her worrying about what she has to prove to me. I can only encourage her to share it so that I, or her colleagues, can validate her and honor her work towards mastery.

I know there are some that are reading this and probably thinking that having all educators in a district operating this way is some kind of work of fiction based in a utopian society. *This all sounds great, but what about that ONE educator I know that just doesn't take the initiative on anything? You're telling me that they shouldn't be held accountable?!* Well, that would depend on where you believe the accountability is coming from.

I would argue that if you are a classroom teacher, your students hold you accountable every day. If you are working in a business where you work directly with your client base, face-to-face, every day, then you are essentially held accountable by your clients. Students tell you in a variety of ways if you are being an effective educator or not, although not always directly or explicitly. You may not even be listening to them, but they're telling you with every eye-roll, every sigh, every discouraged question to see if they're doing it right because they're afraid of not being compliant. Does that sound familiar regarding professional development? The feedback we receive about traditional PD is similar to that of traditional teaching. Those who we serve hold us accountable.

However, if you are one that believes accountability comes from those in administrator roles, then you have most likely adopted a top-down mentality. If there are "reluctant" educators in your building, I would argue…

1. That educator, most likely, hasn't been in a true adult learning environment where autonomy was encouraged, supported, and sustained, but instead has dealt with accountability and compliance for the majority of their career. I have an educated hunch that *more* accountability isn't going to fix that.
2. Why not deal with these singular cases in a singular manner? Why apply the blanket of accountability to all the educators in your district? Even the ones that are already professionally driven, like the 25-year veteran in my example? If you move towards a more Professionally Driven model, blanket forms of accountability won't be necessary.

Evaluations are a very common form of accountability in education. In most states, every educator must be evaluated: teachers evaluated by principals, principals evaluated by the superintendent, and superintendent evaluated by school boards. This directly implies that accountability comes from top down. Rarely do you see a classroom teacher handing out an evaluation form to students in order to get explicit student feedback. It's even more rare for a principal to do the same in order to get feedback from teachers.

I understand that evaluations are required in some states, but are formal evaluations necessary in a process of true autonomous learning, or are they in place to emphasize accountability? I will let you come to your own conclusion based on how your district uses them. However, I have had districts ask if they can tie in the existing mandatory evaluation forms to the Professionally Driven model. It makes sense. The required Individualized Learning Plans (other states may call it something else) that are used as a part of evaluations seem to be similar to a Professionally Driven learning journey. Why require an adult learner to do two separate goals/journeys? Seems like "another thing" then, doesn't it? But this is where we see the grey area. *Can I intrinsically move forward on a learning journey if I know I will be evaluated in the end?* I would say it depends on how the evaluator treats the evaluation of that learning journey.

In the state of Iowa, each teacher is to be evaluated by their building principal. Part of that evaluation is their Individualized Learning Plan. In a few of the districts I work with, the building principal wishes to tie the Individualized Learning Plan with the Professionally Driven journey. Essentially, it's a form that must be filled out by the teacher and the principal and then goes in a file for that teacher. It's the mandate or the "have-to." The Professionally Driven journey is the "want-to."

So if I hear a principal wishes to marry the two together, the grey area becomes, *Does the principal put more emphasis on the **have-to** or the **want-to**?* If the principal wishes to put more emphasis on the Professionally Driven journey, then I would have no problem with him or her tying the Individualized Learning Plan and the Professionally Driven journey together. In one district I work with, the principal does just this. First of all, the principal is going on his own Professionally Driven journey and being more of a lead-learner, not an authoritarian. Second, when it comes time to fill out the evaluation, he treats it as an instructional coaching opportunity:

- Tell me about your journey so far?
- What have you been learning?
- What phase are you in?
- How has this process changed your thinking so far?
- Is there anything I can do to support you on your journey?

The formality of filling out the form is then completed and filed. The principal does not use it as an opportunity to chastise teachers for taking too long to move through their journey or saying he doesn't agree with their topics and thinks they should switch. The grey area becomes more clear through the quality of the conversation: does it feel more top-down or is it more cooperative? The conversation had during the formal evaluation can be more meaningful when it stems from an intent of support and encouragement.

Very rarely is the word "accountability" used with positive connotations in education. The action of implementing an accountability piece can stymie any autonomous process and reinforce the idea of a top-down mentality.

3. TOP-DOWN MENTALITY

I've referenced to this a few times in this book already, but I feel it's worth giving it its own section because of its relation to sustainable autonomy. I also don't want any administrator to feel that I am "calling them out." There are many great administrators who adopt the mindset of lead-learner or see their role as educator as well. This is not pointing a finger at any *person* and their role within a district. It's pointing a finger at the *mentality* itself, which can be adopted by anyone in any role.

In terms of the classroom, the top-down mentality can be adopted very easily by the teacher in leading instruction: *I control the content and how I assess that content; therefore, I control the knowledge input and output.* Now read those last two sentences again, but this time put it in the context of leading a school building and professional development. As you see, a principal could adopt the same phrasing. Or on an even larger scale, a curriculum director or superintendent may adopt the same thinking for whole-district PD initiatives. Basically, go as high up on the rungs of school district positions (according to contract descriptions), and you could see where the mentality could trickle all the way down. This could lead to problems at *both* ends of the ladder.

Top-Down Mentality (Administrator Perspective)

When considering a top-down mentality from the administrator perspective, it's important to mention that administrators usually have to deal with accountability even at the state level. State mandates and legislation usually emphasize the accountability measures that administrators have to follow, and at no fault of the administrator, this can lead to a negative use of accountability at the district or building level. This usually includes statements like, "You need to meet goal (X) by (this date) or (this will be the result)." Statements like these leave no room for autonomy.

It's the job of an administrator to use data to find areas that need to be improved. Once they identify an area that needs improvement, the "initiative" is laid out. The assumption is others will follow. And when they don't, or become "reluctant," then accountability is used in a way that better suits a model of compliance. This is referenced in my *Training vs. Learning* chart in Chapter 3. It can lead to frustration for everyone involved. Administrators feel frustrated when teachers don't see the same need to change, and teachers feel frustrated because someone else is telling them they need to change, though they may not buy into it.

Then came Knoster, Villa, and Thousand's "Framework for Thinking About Systems Change" from their work *Restructuring for Caring and Effective Education: Piecing the Puzzle Together* (2000, pp. 93-128). In the chart below, you can see there are five categories that need to be taken into consideration when leading effective change in education: *Vision*, *Skills*, *Incentives*, *Resources*, and *Action Plan*.

A Framework for Thinking about Systems Change

Adapted from Knoster, Villa, Thousand (2000)
From "Restructuring for caring and effective education: piercing the puzzle together (pp. 93-128)

Vision	Skills	Incentives	Resources	Action Plan	= Result
	+ Skills	+ Incentives	+ Resources	+ Action Plan	= Confusion
Vision +		+ Incentives	+ Resources	+ Action Plan	= Anxiety
Vision +	Skills +		+ Resources	+ Action Plan	= Resistance
Vision +	Skills +	Incentives +		+ Action Plan	= Frustration
Vision +	Skills +	Incentives +	Resources +		= False Starts
Vision +	Skills +	Incentives +	Resources +	Action Plan	= Change

The framework is easy enough to understand. All five are needed in order to get the result we are looking for: **Change**. Could the *Change* in Knoster, Villa, and Thousand's chart be the same *Change* that Guskey refers to in his model of effective PD? I'll leave that one for you to ponder and conclude for yourself.

However, if you are missing one of these five pieces, you can see the result. I have seen this chart referenced in many trainings I've attended. I've even seen it used by administrators at the school district level as, I assume, a persuasive device to gain buy-in for the current initiative. But here is where this chart becomes problematic for me: the **Incentives** category.

As I mentioned in the previous chapter on Motivation, the idea of using incentives is based on extrinsic motivation and is often short-term, assuming that the word "incentives" is being used in the same context that Pink lays out in his book. That means that this framework for *change* is really looking for *short-term* change. What I also find problematic is when I hear frustrated administrators say, "We've worked hard to put all the pieces in place, so we should be seeing *Change*, but we are still experiencing *Resistance*." Find the row that results in Resistance. Notice what piece is missing? *Incentives*. Does that mean the district should sweeten the incentives? If you're looking for short-term change, maybe. So if a district works tirelessly to put all these pieces in place in order to create *Change*, why are they still seeing Resistance? With everything that I've laid out up to this point, I would conclude the reason is that *Change* is being identified and administered in a top-down format. Therefore, methods of extrinsic motivation are used to guide people on a path created for them, leading to negative uses of accountability when extrinsic incentives don't work. The use of such accountability stifles any kind of development for growth mindset and even conditions PD participators to become more fixed in their mindset.

Top-Down Mentality (Participant Perspective)

The top-down mentality can also cause problems for the participants of professional development. When participants of professional development are conditioned to have the initiative laid out for them, they can quickly become disgruntled when the path is not clear. To illustrate this, I'll use an example from my own classroom.

In my last few years of teaching in the classroom, I began to implement flipped learning. It was a focus for my literature review in graduate school, and it forever changed my classroom for the better. It was something that I was drawn to for one major reason: I was able to push the lower-levels of Bloom's Taxonomy out of my classroom and put the onus on the students to frontload. This allowed us to operate in the upper-levels of Bloom's during our face-to-face class time, almost every day, for a school year.

When I began flipping my learning environment, though, I received the greatest pushback from my straight "A" students. In fact, I even had one junior girl stomp her foot in frustration and say out loud, "Why can't you just tell me what I need to know for the test?!" They were frustrated that I wasn't simply giving them content to digest and regurgitate in the lower-levels of Bloom's. In other words, *I wasn't giving them the clear path to be compliant.* Instead, I was asking students (participants) to be more active with their learning. The frustration that the student expressed in my classroom is the same frustration I hear from professional development participants when something is not clearly laid out for them. No participant wants to be labeled as "lazy," "reluctant," or even "non-compliant." At least not educators that I've worked with.

When a top-down mentality is adopted at both ends of the ladder, it does not bode well for a Professionally Driven journey and becomes even more difficult to move away from traditional professional development. The professional development creators are hesitant to relinquish control and the participants don't want to feel that they are not being compliant. For both, this is scary as hell. I use that phrasing because it most accurately describes the severity in confusion I see when I suggest an alternative system like my Professionally Driven model.

I know I sound like I'm generalizing or being over-dramatic, but I literally get the same facial expressions from educators when I say, "If your current PD is not meeting the learning needs for everyone, then let's scratch this whole traditional PD model and move towards a Professionally Driven model." Eyes are either squinty, attempting to understand the concept or wide because I have just put them in a fight-or-flight moment. Both the PD creators and participants have been put in an unfamiliar situation. I am asking them to think about their roles differently. They are no longer creators and participants, but *all active learners*. I can also begin to hear their responses to that fight-or-flight moment in the form of either affirmation of changing what isn't working or excuses as to why they think it won't work.

- "This is exactly what we need."
- "I don't know if this is doable."
- "I love the fact that all educators are driving their own learning."
- "So, they're just picking topics willy-nilly?"
- "This will help drive passion."
- "We give them a list of topics to choose from, right?"

You can easily see which phrases would indicate Fight and which ones would indicate Flight.

Now, I know I have just dropped a hint of hypocrisy, because it sounds like any fight-or-flight moment when change is suggested, even a top-down model. But I do not offer my Professionally Driven model unless it is identified by the district that the current form of professional development is not working. If a district has identified a *weakness*, such as their current form of traditional PD, then I merely present to them a model that could replace their current, ineffective one with something that is more effective. Many school districts start off with the model, offering a portion of the PD time. Notice I let the district identify the weak spot, not me, and that identification comes from teachers *and* administrators. If both groups are not willing to admit that their current form of PD is a weak spot, then the process of replacing it or supplementing it will not happen with fidelity. People aren't willing to change what they don't perceive as an area in need of change. The district needs to be autonomous in determining what isn't working before any suggestions of change can be made.

Falsely Labeling Leadership

Another idea that becomes problematic in terms of top-down mentality is falsely labeling **leadership**. I can see how a person at the administration level who adopts the top-down mentality could easily confuse that with "being a leader." Their job is to identify areas of potential improvement on a building or district scale, then develop ways to improve it. They're just doing their job, right? But you can see where the onslaught of problems that have already been mentioned could occur: Administrator purposes steps necessary to change building/district weakness > rest of staff may or may not buy-in > the initiative is put in place > staff does what it takes to be compliant > some that are resistant despite the incentives are then charged with accountability pieces > these teachers become more resistant than when they started. And this just continues with the next initiative and so on. All the while, the administrator becomes increasingly frustrated, because they thought they were just performing their role as a leader. I've spoken with administrators who have stated something similar to this with exasperation.

When faced with such resistance, I've even heard some administrators say, "Well, I'll just have to lay it out like it is and that's just how it will have to be!" Top-down leadership works very well when you have a solid group of compliers in a well-structured business model, but we're dealing with adult learners in a system of education. Those two roles, in their purest forms—*compliers* and *learners*—cannot coexist. They are a dichotomy that has been referred to as such by too many educational experts to reference here. And I would argue that the fundamental difference between these two is the mindset approach towards the action of listening. This was an idea that forever changed my mindset about leadership, and it all started in high school.

Leaders Lead by Listening

When I was a sophomore in high school, my guidance counselor approached me in the hall one day and said, "Congratulations, you and Alexis have been chosen by the teachers to attend a leadership symposium." I was confused when he told me this, because I hadn't even known the symposium existed. We were never told that this was being decided or even what to expect at this so-called symposium. All our counselor did was stop Alexis and me in the hall, tell us that we would miss school on Friday, handed us a sheet of paper with the itinerary, and told us to wear comfortable clothes. Our friends also thought it was weird when we mentioned it to them, and they did not envy us when they saw that we had to meet a charter bus at 5:30 a.m. However, that day ended up having a very lasting impact on me for many reasons, but one in particular.

We got on the bus, barely awake, with about 25 other male/female pairs of Sophomores from other schools who also knew very little about what the day would entail. By 8:00 a.m., we finally made our destination: Camp Dodge, an Army base in Johnston, IA. This is where the change for me occurred.

The first part of the day consisted of us sitting in a lecture hall and listening to a gentleman deliver a presentation on leadership. Parts of the presentation that I remember vividly include watching a volunteer student attempt to fill a glass bowl of varying sized rocks in order to fit all of them. The big rocks represented big issues that may come up in our lives while the little rocks represented other aspects of our daily life. In order to make everything fit, we can't pile the large rocks first, then dump the smaller rocks on top or vice versa. We have to try to fill all the gaps between big rocks with little ones as we build to the top. A visual representation for how we construct our own lives.

My favorite part of that morning, though, and perhaps the most effective, was when the speaker used a scene from one of my favorite movies of all time, *Dead Poets Society*. The scene was when Mr. Keating (Robin Williams) takes the boys to the trophy case and asks them to lean in and listen to those that have come before them as the camera cuts to pictures of former athletic teams who have achieved greatness in some fashion: "Carpe diem. Seize the day, boys. Make your lives extraordinary." I soaked in these words, *Carpe Diem*, and still continue to use it as my mantra today. Immediately after the clip, the gentleman asked us all, "What does that clip have to do with leadership?" Of course, there was a pause. I'm assuming this guy was a teacher, because his wait time was incredible. Eventually, responses began to chime in:

- "We need to set goals and go for them."
- "We need to make the most of every opportunity out there."
- "We can't sit back and be passive and let time pass us by."
- "We need to always strive to make ourselves better," etc.

This gentleman, who had led us all morning with similar activities, didn't discredit any of our remarks but instead nodded at each one and replied, "OK," until we exhausted all ideas. Once he felt all had had an equal opportunity to share (another reason I believe he was a teacher by day), he then said, "So all of your responses focused on you, the leader. But what did the teacher instruct these boys to do *before* they were told to Carpe Diem?" No answer. He rewound the tape to the beginning of the clip, played it again, and paused immediately after it was stated. One student raised his hand. "Lean in and listen."

The speaker smiled in approval and replied, "Exactly. Leaders don't lead by talking, they lead by listening. They're the ones willing to listen to those around them when others won't. Sure, you want to Carpe Diem and make your lives extraordinary, but how do you empower others to do the same? That's leadership. The greatest compliment that you can give anyone is to let them know that you listened." We then did a couple of listening activities in pairs where we had to share information about ourselves. The person listening had to reply with a detail that would indicate to the other person that they had been listening, followed by a question about what the speaker had said. At the end of the activity, the instructor asked us, "How did you feel when the other person included a detail that showed they listened and asked questions wanting to know more?"

One student replied, "I felt valued. Like they genuinely cared about me."

To further understand the importance of listening as a leader, after a lunch break, we went outside to some obstacle courses in teams of six where we had to complete certain tasks, but each required us to work together as a team in order to complete them. It required us to communicate in a way that included listening to one another, acknowledging one another, problem-solving together, and utilizing each other's strengths. All classic elements of effective actionable teamwork. It was also an exercise that made me realize that we *all* had to function like leaders in order to complete the tasks, not just *one* person. Everyone was active in the problem-solving, the execution, the mistake-making, and the celebration when done. No one person in the group was passive and simply waited to be told what to do. No one actively decided to be the passive and compliant participant. We were operating in an environment where *all* were empowered to be active thinkers, learners, and leaders.

The long bus ride home that night was full of contemplation on the idea of leadership, and how the day had really flipped my original thinking. To this day, the whole experience—being chosen, the journey there, and the journey back—seems odd, but my time spent at Camp Dodge that day forever shaped my ideas and definitions of leadership. I realized it's a label bestowed upon you by others through your actions, the main one being your ability to listen to others. By that definition, anyone is worthy of the title, not just those in higher positions. However, the ones in higher positions have the greatest influence on the environment and its ability to empower all in the group to be leaders. In other words, administrators in a district have the greatest influence on an environment that emphasizes *You listen to me* vs. *I'll listen to you*. One emphasizes top-down while the latter emphasizes bottom-up.

While the trip to the leadership symposium was a personal story, I think you may be able to start seeing some connections that I am trying to make to professional development:

- Does your current professional development value all voices/needs?
- Does your professional development encourage and offer the appropriate time and setting for everyone to stop and listen to one another?
- Does your current professional development allow educators to figure out how to manage the various-sized rocks in their professional lives, or does it feel to educators like another *big* rock?
- Does everyone in your district listen to one another, acknowledge one another, overcome problem-solving together, and utilize each other's strengths?
- Is everyone in your district **active** in the problem-solving, the execution, the mistake making, and the celebration when done?
- Is everyone in your district operating in an environment where ALL are empowered to be active thinkers, learners, and **leaders**?
- How often are those involved in your professional development leaning in to listen to one another and recognize each other?

Notice that I did not direct these questions to any one particular role in your district, because that responsibility should not fall on one person. These are questions for anyone involved in professional development to reflect on, because they should apply to all. The label of *leader* is not one that we get to give ourselves. It is a label that is bestowed upon us by our peers through our actions, including the act of listening. Once you have decided to include everyone in the Professionally Driven process, the next step is to provide long-term sustainability.

WHAT IS SUSTAINABLE?

We've looked at what can kill sustainability in education, but it might be instructive to observe the word in a non-educational context. Many people are familiar with the words sustainable and sustainability, but I think the definition is worth mentioning: *able to be used without being completely used up or destroyed*. That means it's always there, and it stems from a natural place, not artificially created.

One particular area where we see the word used the most is in energy. In the last decade or so, there has been a major push to tap into renewable and sustainable energy rather than depleting other forms of fossil fuels. Solar and wind energy have seen a significant increase in energy contribution. How much of an increase is not as important as how they are tapping into these two sources. From various forms of wind turbines to windows that can now be made up of translucent solar panels, the ways to capture this energy and transform it is increasing by the year. An Idaho company has even debuted solar panel sidewalks that can be walked on and intend to one day have solar panel roads. The point is, people are finding many ways to tap into an energy source that is always there. The question then is, *What is the energy source that professional development could tap into in order to make it more sustainable?* I'm sure when I initially ask that, some may think of times when professional development has been fun or exciting. During these times, the energy seems to be very high. Now, whether it was a professional development that was gamified or even a district mini-conference or Edcamp, is this a high energy that can be sustained? Possibly, but it seems these forms of professional development are built on what I call **artificial sustainability**. It's sustainability that has to be maintained with other high levels of energy and effort.

Think about the work that goes into gamifying PD, organizing a mini conference in your district, and coordinating other structures where those participating are highly energized. They take a lot of preparation, organizing, effort, and energy. That means artificial sustainability can be maintained, but it's going to take a lot of work and energy to do so. Artificial sustainability also means that *the energy that is being tapped into wasn't there in the first place*. It has to be summoned, created, or generated. Whereas in the case of solar and wind, those two sources were already there. This is what I call **natural sustainability**. The energy was always there, we just had to find ways to tap into it.

If we apply this same idea to professional development, then the question becomes, *What is the natural source of* **energy** *that has always existed, but we just need to figure out how to tap into it?* To find the answer, we need to think like a caveman.

THINK LIKE A CAVEMAN

To answer the question *What is sustainable?* we need to go back before formal education even took shape. No, *much* farther back. Think back to the time of cavemen, when **curiosity** drove much, if not all of our learning. I like using the following image, which is of a diorama located in the National Museum of Mongolian History in Ulaanbaatar, Mongolia.

Even cavemen knew how to learn. They didn't need classrooms or textbooks to be told how to learn. They would naturally see something that wasn't quite working the way they wanted it to. They would then try other tools, possibly using the bone of an animal in a way that was not previously used before. They might have to use trial-and-error before they got it to work correctly. Once it did, they made it a part of their daily life. They also might tell other cavemen in the area about their new discovery. And on top of all that, they wished to share that knowledge to a bigger audience by painting it on cave walls. I argue that this is the most natural and sustainable form of learning, which is why I use it as the basis for the four phases of a learning journey: Research, Integrate, Reflect, Share.

From the earliest days of cavemen to more modern days, we can see this sustainable form of learning also producing a natural form of energy that I feel we can tap into. Sugata Mitra proved this with his Hole-in-the-Wall project. Mitra traveled to a village in Northern India to mount a computer with internet access into a wall. Mitra provided basic instructions on how it works and such, but other than that, he gave the villagers no real guidance on what or how to learn. Instead, kids became naturally curious. They began to ask questions. They began to learn how to problem-solve and even learn English—all without the direct instruction of an adult, badges, extrinsic motivators, or accountability. Once the experiment had grown to other places across India, students were teaching themselves biotechnology.

Mitra tapped into a natural form of learning that has always existed, it was just done with a different tool. The computer allowed learning to happen at a faster rate than it did in the caveman days, but the same process happened nonetheless. Steve Jobs famously referred to the computer as "a bicycle for the brain": a tool that allows learning to occur more efficiently. Mitra went on to win TED Talk's yearly one million dollar award to build a school that exists only in the Cloud.

Curiosity, the natural sense of wonder and possibility that we were born with and has allowed us to adapt as a species for eons, is the natural source of energy that we could potentially tap into. It's necessary in order to drive natural sustainability when it comes to professional development rather than conjuring other forms of artificial sustainability. *If we believe that we are born with it, does it ever fully leave?* I don't think so. However, it certainly can lie dormant due to our surroundings and environment. If our surroundings don't encourage us to summon our natural sense of curiosity, then we can become conditioned to suppress it. I think the idea of compliance as a prerequisite for training does a fairly effective job of this, for all the reasons that I have already stated.

So rather than pushing away, ignoring, suppressing, or rejecting that natural energy of learning, why not tap into it and use it? Move away from formal and systematic methods of training disguised as "learning," and replace them with a model for adults that *starts with learning first*, then builds around it.

TRADITIONS = SUSTAINABILITY

Often when I think about the idea of sustainability and ask myself, *What makes (X) sustainable?* I come back to the idea of **traditions**. Traditions can exist on a large or small scale. They can take place within a whole culture or within a household. Some individuals even create their own traditions. But no matter what, most traditions are sustainable. This is usually because people give value to them, and that value is made up of a few components:

- **Time**: Traditions usually take place on the same day of the week, day of the month, time of day, etc. For example, it's considered tradition for some college basketball programs to start their first practice at midnight on the first day of the opening season since that is technically the earliest you can practice. Fittingly, it's called Midnight Madness. This then becomes a yearly tradition. Holidays can even be considered traditions since they take place the same day every year.

- **People**: Most traditions, though not necessarily all, involve people gathering. Again, this could be a small group or a very large group. Usually, the purpose for gathering is significant enough for people to keep showing up time and time again, even if it may not be the same people every time. In the case of watching fireworks on the 4th of July, people gather to celebrate a date and what occurred on that date, but people also gather to watch fireworks. Whether at their house (legally) or in the city park, the fireworks are what draws the crowd. And when people gather, they converse, catch up, share, etc. Now, I will say that fireworks is an example of *artificial sustainability* that can be sustained, but it takes money, volunteers, and time to set up, launch, and clean up. If those were not in place, fireworks would not be maintained.

But people find fireworks valuable enough to continue gathering. Therefore, the energy is put into maintaining them.

- **The "thing" being valued**: It's not enough to simply have people gathering on a recurring date and/or time. There needs to be the reason, or the "thing" that everyone gives value to. Coming together to shoot fireworks gives value to our country's independence. Holding a basketball practice at midnight of opening season gives value to the sport, its athletes, and the work necessary to succeed. Any tradition that has been sustained for long periods of time has always centered on something that is being valued by the group of people.

These three ingredients—time, people, and the "thing" worth valuing—are components necessary to starting and sustaining a tradition. In order to make professional development feel like a sustainable tradition, I highly recommend establishing these three pieces and protecting each one as something sacred. Without one, you don't have a self-sustaining tradition that everyone takes part in or values.

In the next chapter, I propose a model that contains all three ingredients in order to build and sustain a model of professional development that feels like a positive tradition for the culture of your district.

QUESTIONS TO CONSIDER FOR SUSTAINABLE AUTONOMY AND PROFESSIONAL DEVELOPMENT...

- Are *all* people in your district empowered to have the opportunity to be labeled a **leader** by their peers?
- Is your current professional development a model of **learning** or a model of **compliance**?
- Does your current professional development feel more like "**yearly initiatives**"?
- Are learners **active** in the professional development process or are they **passive**? Is this due to the current model of professional development being used?
- Does your district focus on **accountability**, or rather creating a learning environment that doesn't need it?
- Is a **top-down mentality** being adopted within your district?
- Does your current form of professional development rely primarily on continual "buy-in" from participants, or is it a system truly focused on empowerment?
- Does your current form of professional development rely on **artificial sustainability** or **natural sustainability**?
- Does your current form of professional development feel like a **tradition** that includes *time*, *people*, and *a "thing" to be valued?*

PROFESSIONALLY DRIVEN EDUCATOR
LIZ HILL
High School Math Teacher

At Kee High in Lansing, IA, Liz chose to finally embark on the flipped learning journey as an educator. However, in her Professionally Driven process, she wasn't getting the results she was looking for with one class while her other class was seeing positive effects on learner outcomes. In her own words, hear how autonomy drove the journey and the courage to try a new instructional strategy.

I began my Professionally Driven journey soon after Jarod led my school through a training seminar. I was invigorated by this process to know that I had autonomy in my professional development and that I was going to be supported throughout the journey. I had been debating implementing a flipped classroom into my high school classes for years and was originally interested in the flipped classroom because I wanted to be able to increase the amount of class time my students spent in the higher level Bloom's objectives. Also, the ability for students to re-watch lessons and accommodate the learning pace of all students was appealing. As part of the Research phase of the Professionally Driven model, I began to research flipped classrooms. I attended some conferences about flipped learning, researched statistics from instructors that had implemented the flipped classroom, and read about different classrooms using this teaching strategy. I discovered that this flipped learning process can look different based on content area. After concluding that the research behind flipped learning was positive for learner outcomes, I decided to implement the idea into my high school Algebra I classroom.

The first step in the Integration phase was learning how to make videos. I used Screencast-o-matic software the district provided and utilized our technology coordinator during PD tech sessions to learn how to make and upload the videos to a class YouTube site. At first the video-making process was tedious. I tried searching for ready-made videos for each section but found that was more work than to overcome the barrier of seeing and hearing myself on video. In the beginning there was no editing of the videos, but as I became more comfortable with the process, I used the editing feature more often. The process of making the videos really helped me become a better instructor because I was forced to not only watch myself but also condense the material to keep the video under ten minutes.

When it was time to implement, I spent the first chapter demonstrating to kids how to go through the process. This included watching the video together, pausing to take notes, and replaying if necessary. The next chapter, the students did this independently in class, and I eventually set them free to do it on their own, as homework. This then allowed the students time during class to work through application problems that challenged them to higher levels of Bloom's taxonomy spectrum.

The Reflection phase of my Professionally Driven journey helped me to fine tune my instruction. Finding a good way to collect data was something I didn't think about until part way through the process so my data was based on grades, classroom pacing, and student feedback. In the beginning of implementing the flipped classroom, the process worked well. Over time, the flipped classroom did not work as well for my students and reflecting on the process helped me to understand why. I found it interesting that while the flipped classroom was successful with one group of students and not with another, it reinforced the idea that I need to continue to look at each class individually and decide what will work with each group.

Ultimately, the Professionally Driven model gave me the encouragement to take my instructional practices to the next level because I had CHOICE of my topic and designated time to work on it. I would not have been able to implement the idea as quickly without the district-allocated time and easy access to technology support in the building if I needed it. I was able to share my journey during the Sharing phase, and this made it easier to connect to and collaborate with other educators regarding implementation, successes and frustrations of the flipped classroom. I am excited to take another journey through the Professionally Driven model using all that I learned from my first experience.

CHAPTER 5
THE PROFESSIONALLY DRIVEN MODEL

It's not handing educators another "have-to." It's putting in place the necessary supports so the "want-to" can come to fruition.

Up to this point, I have laid out the reasons, or the "why" to shift from a traditional PD model to a Professionally Driven model. In order to empower all adult learners in your district to be professionally driven, we must develop a learning model that fosters a growth mindset, intrinsic motivation, and sustainable autonomy. I call these **The Big Three to be PD**, and they are the basis of the Professionally Driven model. The image below is one that I use with districts that emphasizes these three components from chapters 2, 3, and 4.

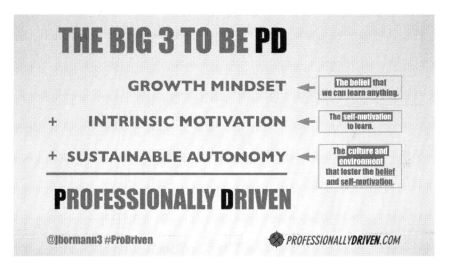

When presented with this equation, it shows that all three components are absolutely necessary. Leaving one out can make professional development feel incomplete, or even worse, a model that still clutches to the heels of compliance. While two of these may be in place, the one that is often missing is **sustainable autonomy**. Take a moment to reflect on your current professional development. Does it empower *ALL* adult learners to have a growth mindset as described in Chapter 2? Does it empower ALL adult learners to be intrinsically motivated as in Chapter 3? And does it empower ALL adult learners to be autonomous with their learning, and is that autonomy *sustained* as we discussed in Chapter 4? If not, then perhaps it's time to consider a model that empowers all adult learners in your district to be Professionally Driven.

In the last three chapters I explained **why** we need to shift away from traditional PD, and in this chapter the focus is on **how** to implement a Professionally Driven model. I have alluded to parts of this chapter already in some of the previous chapters, but now I will explain them more explicitly in order to clearly bring all the pieces together. Think of this chapter as the "nuts and bolts" of the Professionally Driven model that supports all three of the components mentioned above.

THE PROCESS OF THE MODEL

1. **Find the Weak Spot**: Before you can begin your learning journey, you must first find the weak spot in your instruction. Again, this can include any method you may already be using (like PLC's) or other methods that may include looking at data. However, in Chapter 2, I offer another method to determine weaknesses within our instruction. (Chp. 2, *Growth Mindset*)

2. **Research**: Once you identify your weakness, you must begin turning it into a strength. Go out and seek better instructional methods that are more effective than what you were previously using. And remember, your research does not have to come from peer-reviewed journal articles. (Chp. 3, *Intrinsic Motivation*)

3. **Integrate**: Once you have all the information you need to turn your weakness into a strength, do it. However, the big question is, *What will you look for to determine whether or not it's working*? (Chp. 3, *Intrinsic Motivation*)

4. **Reflect**: Once you feel you are using the new instructional strategy with fidelity and seeing the results you were hoping for, share your journey *within your district*. (Chp. 3, *Intrinsic Motivation*)

5. **Share**: New learning should be shared. Once you've shared *inside* your district, share *outside* your district. Present at conferences, publish a video to YouTube, or blog and share it

via social media. Connecting to a larger learning community is what it's all about. (Chp. 3, *Intrinsic Motivation*)

6. **Tech Sessions/Trainings**: These are available per request. Only those needing the training are encouraged to attend and can do so at any point on their learning journey. (Chp. 3, *Intrinsic Motivation*)

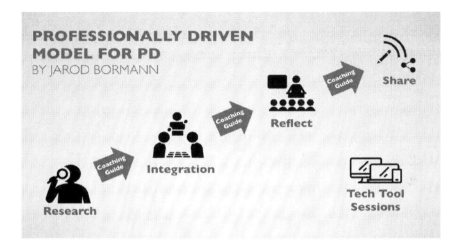

MAKE THE PROCESS PERSONAL

While the phases of the journey may seem pretty straightforward, I recommend using a local/personalized analogy to help make the model feel more personalized for each district. This Professionally Driven model can be applied to any school district at any level, but it's through making the process personal that I've seen a school really take ownership of it.

You might recall back to Chapter 3 where I make the connection between a learning journey and the Hero's Journey. Joseph Campbell proved to us that the narrative of the Hero's Journey is embedded in the human experience and can be found anywhere. Well, the learning journey is no different. It's a process, and that process can be tied to a school district.

One school I work with has a hawk as their mascot (tinyurl.com/keehighpd). We were brainstorming how the learning phases might tie into the idea of hawks. Once I did a little more research on the developmental cycle of a hawk, the phases became very apparent:

- Hatchling - Research
- Fledgling - Integration
- Adult Hawk - Reflection
- Soaring - Sharing
- The Nest - Tech Sessions

This analogy ties in well because you truly feel like that independent adult hawk when you get the chance to reflect within your district. Not only that, when you eventually share outside the district, you truly are soaring to the point where you feel there are no boundaries with your learning.

Another district I work with is located in a town that has a river running through it. The river is a tourist attraction and a centerpiece for the community, so we brainstormed how to connect an analogy to the river. Several ideas came about, including the various bodies of water that flow from one to the next (i.e. *creek > stream > river > delta > ocean*). This seemed to work, but it just didn't resonate with those on the planning team. We then jumped to the idea of using the mascot, the Warriors, but nothing was generated from that either. We then went back to the river, but instead of focusing on the river, someone suggested the bridge. There is a large, historic limestone arch bridge that spans the river and connects one half of the town to the other. This analogy seemed to click for everyone once we figured out the phases.

- Plan - Research
- Construction - Integration
- Ribbon Cutting - Reflection
- Bridge Opening - Sharing
- Materials - Tech Sessions

I feel this analogy is very appropriate for what we are attempting to do with individuals' Professionally Driven journeys: when you discover a gap in your instruction, figure out how to build a bridge to take you to the next step in your journey.

There are several other analogies that can be used. From a treasure map (Postville Pirates: tinyurl.com/postvillepd) to the process of baking (St. Joseph's School: tinyurl.com/stjoespd), these four phases can be found in many aspects of our everyday lives. This also shows that these phases always have been, and always will be, deeply embedded in the human experience. The local/personalized analogy is what draws us into that process and drives us to connect it to other areas of our lives. It further emphasizes that PD isn't simply something we *do (professional development)*, but it's something we *become (Professionally Driven).*

RECOGNIZING THE LEARNING PROCESS

If the only steps educators took was move through the four phases of the Professionally Driven journey, a few things would most likely occur:

1. Educators will feel lost, because they're not sure which phase they are in.
2. Educators will hit a hurdle and feel like they are just spinning their wheels for no reason.
3. Educators will feel undervalued for the work they are going through.

For these reasons, I feel it is extremely important to recognize each educator's learning process. To do this, I recommend each school develops a *recognition piece* that honors an educator's progression from one phase to the next. This recognition piece could be tied to the local/personalized analogy that the school develops. In the story of Oelwein, their analogy was "Climbing a Mountain." Therefore, the recognition pieces used were flags, much like how climbers use flags to denote reaching the next higher camp on the mountain. However, these recognition pieces aren't simply extrinsic motivators. They do serve a greater purpose.

RECOGNITION OF THE PROCESS

As educators, we are instructed to celebrate student learning. I feel the same should be for adult learning. That is why I recommend holding some kind of recognition ceremony for educators who move from one phase into the next. For example, when an educator completes the Research phase, they receive their first recognition piece. Then, once they complete the Integration phase, they turn in their first recognition piece and receive the next one. This continues again after the Reflection phase. However, once they complete their first learning journey by completing the Sharing Phase, they get to *keep* that recognition piece.

This turning in and handing out of recognition pieces is done at a Recognition Ceremony. While this may seem "cheesy" and cause reservation for some, I highly recommend that it have the atmosphere of a celebration: play ceremonial music, project slides that show each educator's name with the phase they have completed and what their topic is, and applaud one another. Whatever you do, make it feel special and keep it consistent. By keeping it consistent, you make it feel like a positive tradition, and positive traditions turn into positive cultures. Not only that, traditions help strengthen the sustainability of the Professionally Driven model in your district. In the previous chapter, we saw how traditions can play a key role in the sustainability of autonomy. If educators are recognized for their work, whether individually or in small collaborative groups, it honors the process of learning, not just the finished product.

ADJUSTING FOR DISTRICT SIZE

Coming together as a district and celebrating the learning of one another is easier to do in a smaller school district that may only have one or two buildings within close proximity of one another. In a larger school district with several buildings and many teachers, it can be difficult to bring everyone in the district together. In this case, it is up to the district to decide whether you wish to celebrate as a whole or on a building-by-building basis. I also leave it up to the district to decide how often they do the Recognition Ceremony. Some may do the ceremony as soon as educators are ready to move from one phase to the next, or they may wait and do it on a quarterly basis. I have seen this work both ways. It really just depends on the overall size of the district and how close the buildings are to one another, because this affects driving time for educators. But if you are a larger school district and you wish to celebrate on a building-by-building basis, I still recommend that the type of recognition ceremony stay the same. Everyone needs to decide how they are going to properly recognize the educators so it stays consistent from building to building and keeps the idea of a district culture consistent.

PROUD TO PUT ON DISPLAY

As I mentioned, in the early stages of planning with Oelwein, we decided to use flags to recognize the process of learning, because it tied in well with the analogy that we set up. I initially thought that these flags would be something fairly small on a stick, like the

American flags passed out at parades that you see people waving around with one hand. However, when I walked into Superintendent Steve Westerberg's office, I was presented with a very different kind of flag. These flags hung vertically and were approximately 3 feet long. Each flag was attached to a wooden rod and rope, so it can be hung vertically on a wall. I was very impressed to say the least. When I asked Steve why he went with a larger flag, he said something I will never forget: "I wanted something all educators would be proud to put on display." And I couldn't agree more. It was something that I had not considered in this process, and I'm glad he did. "The bigger flags probably cost more, right?" I asked him.

"If every educator in this district is intrinsically motivated to improve instruction, then it's worth every dollar," was his reply. The primary cost is an initial one, though, because educators are turning in the flags before receiving their next one. The only new flags that will need to be purchased in the future are the ones that educators get to keep when they complete the Sharing phase for the first time. However, if an educator completes additional learning journeys, they don't receive additional flags to keep. Instead, they get a button to attach to their flag.  So when an educator retires from the district, they will have a final flag with multiple buttons on it, signifying a career's worth of learning as an educator.

Another school I work with, Central in Elkader, IA, (tinyurl.com/centralcs) uses large 8" round magnets of varying colors to signify the first three phases. These magnets can be displayed on the whiteboards in the front of their rooms or anywhere else they wish. As I mentioned earlier, their analogy is "Building a Bridge to Learning," because of the historic stone-arch bridge that spans the river. Once an educator completes the Sharing Phase at Central, they receive a block of limestone etched with Central's Professionally Driven motto. When they complete the journey again, a mark is etched on their block of limestone. So rather than having multiple blocks of limestone, it's just one that they are proud to put on display in their classroom, marked with the number of journeys completed.

Some educators may choose to not put their recognition piece on display, and that's fine too. They do with it what they wish until it's time to receive the next one. However, we want to be able to recognize all educators on the learning journey that they are defining for themselves.

STRUCTURING TIME FOR THE PROCESS

I hear it all the time from teachers: "I never have enough time." I also hear administrators accusing teachers of using this as an excuse. However, it's a valid issue! I didn't realize how precious time was in the teaching profession until I left the classroom. It was then I realized that when a teacher says, "I don't have time," what they really mean is, "Too much of my time is being dictated by someone else." If you think about it, a teacher's entire day is completely dictated by a very structured bell system. Teachers often joke about finding enough time to even go to the bathroom. This is only slightly humorous, because we know it to be true some days. This dictated time spills over into a teacher's personal life when they must grade or provide feedback on student work outside of the regular school day, and this doesn't include extracurricular coaching responsibilities. To say that time is perhaps the most precious commodity for teachers is an understatement.

Administrators also have busy days dictated by outside factors: parents, scheduling conflicts, student issues, etc. Administrators' time outside of the school day is also taken up by attending extracurricular events. Their day is just as busy as teachers', but isn't quite as dictated or regimented by bells.

So if time is the most precious commodity for both teachers and administrators, a district has to look at the biggest time-wasters. Just like what we did with classroom instruction, when we look at where the weakness is, most districts look at professional development as a weakness, seeing it as the greatest time-waster. If that's the case, then we must admit it is a weakness and replace it with something that values time better.

That is where this Professionally Driven model comes in. We are not looking to add this model to the district's initiatives; we are looking to replace bad professional development with a professional development model that we know works. We know this model supports effective learning for *all* adult learners and educators. Therefore, we need to make sure that we structure the time for it *inside* the contractual professional development time for educators. Don't tell educators the only opportunities they have for their own learning is during what little free time they have. By valuing all educators' time to learn, you are in fact valuing the people in those adult learning roles, both teachers and administrators.

As you begin planning for the Professionally Driven model, you will want to make sure that you structure the proper time. I call the specific contractual professional development time *personalized PD time* or *personalized PD sessions*. The personalized PD time is what allows educators to move through the Professionally Driven model.

REFLECTION PHASE (SHARING INSIDE YOUR DISTRICT)
As noted earlier in this book, the Reflection phase gives educators the opportunity to share their learning within their district. While some educators may opt for creating a video or blog and sharing it within their district, it is still important to also include the option for educators to give a 10-minute TED-style talk to their colleagues or any other option they choose. When, exactly, these presentations take place depends partly on how big of a school district you have.

Smaller districts I work with allot time for the reflection talks at the beginning of personalized PD sessions. These smaller school districts are able to have all educators meet in the same location. In contrast, larger school districts find this difficult due to the fact they have multiple buildings. Maybe your reflection talks take place only within your building. They should then be recorded and shared with the rest of the district. Some districts don't have weekly professional development time already established. These schools could provide time for the reflection talks once per quarter. I would not go any longer than that, because you want people to begin moving to the next phase without waiting for the district to provide the reflection time.

The Reflection phase is also important to schedule because it's the one time we really get to **lean in and listen** to our fellow colleagues and honor them as professionals. I posed the question in Chapter 4 (Sustainable Autonomy): *How often do the adult learners in your district lean in to really listen and acknowledge one another?* This is that opportunity, and the time to do so needs to be protected and kept sacred.

RECOGNITION CEREMONY

The recognition ceremony is another piece that should be done frequently enough for educators to feel that they are moving forward. Most of the school districts I work with do a recognition ceremony whenever educators are ready to move to the next phase. Some school districts that are larger hold the recognition ceremony either once per month or once per quarter. But like the Reflection phase, I would not recommend waiting longer than that to perform the recognition ceremony. My rule of thumb for the recognition ceremony: recognize educators' work when the work is being performed. If you wait any longer, the recognition loses its effect on valuing educators.

PERSONALIZED PD TIME/TECH SESSIONS

The majority of your professional development time in these personalized PD sessions will be dedicated to individual or small group work and/or Tech Sessions. If we were to look back at the idea of *training vs. learning*, you want to make sure that time for both is balanced appropriately. Many school districts that I work with have weekly late starts or early dismissals to allow for professional development time for educators. This adds up to four opportunities of professional development per month at around two hours per week. Out of these four opportunities, I would highly recommend designating, at minimum, one of those sessions for personalized PD time. I realize that is only two hours/month, but added up over a school year, it can total somewhere around 18 hours of personalized PD time that was not originally in the professional development calendar. And if you are at a school that is able to have weekly professional development time, you have the advantage of spreading out those 18 hours over the course of the whole school year. If you are a school district that only provides full-day or half-day professional development sporadically throughout the year, it will be more difficult to implement personalized PD time. I have found that going longer than one month without personalized PD time only impedes the progress of the learning journey. Some educators lose track of where they are on their journey and may lose interest in the journey all together.

Now, there's no rule that says educators are only allowed to work on their Professionally Driven journey during the allotted personalized PD time. However, as I mentioned before, finding that time can be very difficult for an educator. And as a reminder, the term "educator" included both teacher and administrator in this Professionally Driven model. By designating time for the learning at least once per month, with coaching support, you are valuing all educators as professional learners.

Also during the personalized PD time, Tech Sessions can be held. I highly recommend having a designated computer lab or space for the Tech Sessions. Only educators that feel they need the session should attend. Tech Sessions are not mandatory for everyone. Also, these sessions are ~30 minutes usually. That still leaves plenty of time for further work on their Professionally Driven journey if necessary.

For everyone else not in the Tech Session, they are free to keep working through their Professionally Driven journey either individually or in their collaborative group. However, *where* they work is important. I recommend designating a hallway (or two) of classrooms where educators can choose to work. If the place where everyone meets is in the auditorium, have the hallway of classrooms be near the auditorium. Having designated work areas to choose from serves two big purposes:

1. It condenses the area that coaches need to cover in order to check-in with as many educators as possible. If a coach knows that everyone is in these rooms every time, it maximizes their time to be able to connect with each educator rather than roaming all over the building trying to find everyone. This is NOT meant to be an easier "big brother" system of "keeping a sharp eye" on educators and treating them like anything less than professionals (*which should not happen*). It is purely for coaches to be able to provide whatever support educators need on their learning journey in a more timely manner.
2. It prevents educators from becoming easily distracted with all the "other things" that need to get done. Personalized PD time is not simply "work time," which is what I have heard educators initially refer to it as. It's time to really focus on

you and *your learning*. If we said educators can work anywhere they want, as a teacher, I would choose to work in my room. And let's be honest, if I'm in my room with the door closed, that stack of papers that needs grading looks awfully tempting.

I realize it sounds like compliance for me to say, "Educators can't work in their rooms because we can't trust them." That's not it at all. As I've said before, in a compliance model, the path is laid out *for* the educator. In this Professionally Driven model, the path is laid out *by* the educator. So if I am an instructional coach, and I happen to spot an educator who is choosing "work that needs to get done" over their learning journey, that tells me they might not be on the right journey or they may be slightly off course. Or, maybe there are other outside compliance factors that are negatively affecting the personalized PD time. If the educator is truly intrinsically motivated about their journey, they would most likely find their learning journey to be more cognitively engaging than grading papers. If the educator is in the Integration phase and the assignment was part of the formative information that tells them if the new instructional strategy is working or not, then I would say it's OK to continue the work. However, if I were a coach, I wouldn't know this unless I initiated a conversation and asked about their journey.

From time to time, a school district using this Professionally Driven model will get in touch with me and say, "It feels like things are becoming too loose. Almost like it's just free time or a study hall for educators." When I ask how the personalized PD time is structured, almost every time they mention a lack of designated spaces to work. Districts that feel the time is being used and valued properly have those designated spaces, because coaches are able to provide that timely support.

SCHEDULING
Most of the schools I work with have a two-hour late start or early dismissal each week for professional development. In those school districts, this is how we schedule the appropriate amount of personalized PD time if a minimum of two hours/month is offered:

1. Everyone meets in same designated space.
2. Reflection Talks (if there are any): 10-15 minutes.
3. Recognition Ceremony (if there are any to be recognized): 10 minutes or less.
4. Personalized PD Time and/or Tech Session for the remainder of the two hours.

I tell school districts to always have a common place to meet at the very beginning of personalized PD time. This is usually in an auditorium or cafeteria. However, *I recommend making it the same place every time.* This helps to avoid any confusion or wasting precious personalized PD time. You want to reach the point where educators just know that on days of personalized PD sessions, they meet "here." This also helps build on the idea of tradition, which again, also helps establish the idea of sustainability. Like most traditions that we experience in our lives, we know who is meeting, where it is and when.

While it is recommended to offer personalized PD time at least once per month for a minimum of two hours, I work with some school districts that offer it two or three times per month. These schools are seeing a culture of learning develop more quickly than schools that are only offering it once per month. Some educators have been in a professional development model of compliance for *years.* Shifting them to a more active learning process is not going to happen overnight, nor should we expect it to. They simply need to know that this is a model for learning that is not going away or being treated like another "yearly initiative." This is going to take time, and the more frequently you allot personalized PD time, the faster the shift. However, I realize that offering it this frequently is difficult for some schools to do. That is why I only recommend a *minimum* as a rule of thumb for all who are considering this model. The time is ultimately flexible based on the size of your district, other mandates that require *training* time, and your existing professional development schedule for the year.

Now that you have done the leg work of structuring the necessary time for the learning process, and you know how you will properly recognize the learning process, it is time to actually get started.

Getting Started

To go from traditional PD to a more Professionally Driven model in one fell swoop would be too much shock to the system for most. Shifting mindsets like that does not happen overnight. Therefore, I recommend a process of acclimation. Much like bringing a new fish home from the pet store in a small plastic bag, it is recommended to first submerge the whole bag in the new tank of water in order for the two water temperatures to slowly reach the same temperature, *then* release the fish from the small bag into the water tank. Dumping the fish from the small bag of water directly into the larger tank right away is often so much of a temperature shock that the fish cannot adapt quickly enough and risks dying. We don't want this same effect with educators. I'm not saying they'll die from the shock, obviously, but it will be too much for some. They will be moving from passive learning to active learning, and while the educators that are already professionally driven will adapt just fine, others will turn cold and negative if shifted too quickly.

THE TEASER

In order to begin the acclimation process, I first introduce the Professionally Driven model by giving a Teaser presentation. I call it that, because it's very similar to a teaser trailer that you would see for movies. It doesn't show the whole movie, but it's enough to get you hooked and wanting more.

At a professional development session already scheduled in the district calendar, I take 15-25 minutes to essentially present to the staff *What is the Professionally Driven model* and *Why is it more effective than Traditional PD?* I discuss Guskey's model (Chp. 2) and the reasons why traditional PD is considered ineffective (Chp. 1). I will then introduce the four phases of the learning journey (Chp. 3). The goal here is to merely introduce the idea of the model, especially to those that have never really heard of the concept, which is the majority. I do leave time for some large group discussion if needed in order to hear thoughts and at least start a conversation. I don't go into any more detail about what the model will look like for that district specifically. I save that conversation for down the road, usually the following month.

The intent of the Teaser is to ignite a conversation and to hopefully keep that conversation going in the coming month. That month is usually when some teachers will begin to question the model. They may question whether it's something that will truly make a difference, or if it is simply "another thing." In that time, it's up to the administrator, instructional coaches, and myself to assuage any anxiety or frustration that may begin to bubble. This is where the listening and the trust begin to take shape. You will find throughout this entire process that **trust** is essential. If you are in a building where trust is limited or even non-existent, then using this model to empower educators to become Professionally Driven will take longer. Trust is something that that takes effort to gain, maintain, and earn. These initial conversations between teachers, admins, and coaches are the first steps in establishing the necessary tone of trust in your district.

THE REVEAL

When Steve Jobs revealed the iPhone in 2007, the whole world was watching. We may not have been able to get our hands on one that same day, but it was the moment when everyone had the chance to see it and understand what it can do. It was the first time we understood that the internet, mp3 player, and phone could be one device, and he explained how it will make our lives better. While revealing the Professionally Driven model for adult learning does not equate to the iPhone, the purpose of the reveal is similar.

One month (roughly) after the Teaser, we will do the **Reveal**. This is where the staff gets to see the website (or some other kind of central hub) for the first time. Each phase in the journey is described for the educators, simply because there are many questions that come along with something new. You'll also have some educators who are very hesitant to embrace the idea. I think of the movie Goonies when they all gather around the map for the first time in the attic. You have the educators who are adventurous with a more growth mindset who can't wait to start the journey. However, there are those that are more hesitant saying, "I don't know, guys. This sounds like a bad idea," and then they begin to list all the reasons why. For any educators who had slight hesitation prior to The Reveal, their hesitations will only be amplified after The Reveal. Once again, the instructional coaches can communicate with them further in order to assuage their fears.

Being fearful is natural. It's that fight-or-flight response, the one that triggers our second level of Maslow's Hierarchy of Needs: Safety/Security. Therefore, no one should be ashamed for feeling fearful when shifting to a Professionally Driven model. If my kids came to me and said they were afraid of the dark, they obviously will not get over their fear if I simply said to them, "Get over it" or "Deal with it" or "This is just the way it will be." We need to acknowledge that this is something new, and it will take a little time to adjust to, but with support, we'll get there as a community of learners.

Once the Reveal happens, I will usually wait another few weeks before we actually do The Kick-Off. Again, this is so the staff can digest what each phase means, maybe even explore the website that was designed for them. Not all educators will take this initiative and look at the website, and that's OK. Educators are busy. But those educators that are already primed for this kind of learning model will take the initiative. These educators are most likely already professionally driven, and their excitement will flow to others.

It is absolutely essential to create a "central hub" for all things related to your district's Professionally Driven journey. Everyone needs to be able access the Coaching Guide Questions (discussed in the next chapter) and other related material for each phase. This is very similar to a teacher who begins to use a Learning Management System (Schoology, Canvas, Blackboard, etc.) for their flipped learning environment. In fact, one school I worked with used Schoology as their central hub simply because they had it purchased already. We also thought this would be a good way for some educators to begin learning more about utilizing Schoology. But in most cases, someone needs to create a website for the district's Professionally Driven journey. The website also allows for the inclusion of the district's local/personalized analogy they wish to use.

Having something visual, like a website that portrays the district's journey, delivers the message that being Professionally Driven isn't just theoretical or hearsay; it's something that can be done and here's how. It is much like explorers who were the first brave enough to venture out, create maps to show others how to navigate the terrain, and say to them, "You can make it here, too. And if you forge your own path that's not on this map, be sure to add it."

The phases that I have set up in this model very much mimic a journey of learning, and I will often use the word **journey** intentionally when I speak with administrators, instructional coaches, and teachers about becoming professionally driven. The idea of a journey means that when you set forth, you understand that you will not be the same person when get to your destination. There will be unknowns, but you're willing to experience them. My Professionally Driven model is much like a map. For educators hesitant to begin or not sure where to begin, they may need that map, and the Reveal provides that map for the first time. However, once they have gone on enough learning journeys, they will begin blazing their own trails and sharing them with others in the learning community.

THE KICK-OFF

Whether it's your birthday, wedding, opening day for your favorite sport, the most exciting day of the year is when that event finally arrives. Well, for the Professionally Driven journey, the day has arrived. All staff members have had ample opportunities to review what the model looks like and ask any questions they may have. The instructional coaches (and others involved in the PD planning process) have had time to answer those questions and make everyone feel comfortable and ready to start. To start the kick-off, present to the whole staff the process of identifying the weak spot (Chp. 2). I cover this process prior to breaking out into groups so the three filters are clear as they think about their first topic: *1) it should not be "tool-driven" 2) it must be focused on a positive effect on student outcomes 3) it should excite them the most.*

Prior to Kick-Off Day

I ask the administration for a list of the teaching staff. With that list, I try to break up the groups into even numbers, usually about 10 per group, with one person acting as the lead for the group. I don't recommend groups larger than 12 or so, because then it becomes difficult for some to open up about the topic. The lead for the group could be myself, an instructional coach, or a teacher-leader who was a part of the planning process. The objective of the leader in the group is to mainly keep the Professionally Driven topics centered on the three filters. They are also there to facilitate the conversation and invite other people's opinions and voices into the bouncing around of ideas. Administrators are also a part of these groups, because they are establishing their own learning journeys. However, I do *not* have administrators as the "lead" in the group, simply because administrators are evaluators, and I do not want this model to feel evaluative in any way. All educators, both teachers and administrators, are pure **learners** in this model.

I create a Google Doc that has a table with all the educators' names divided into their groups. The second column in that table allows for the educator or the lead facilitator to type in the topic that they came up with. This document is usually titled "Kick-off Document." It serves two purposes: 1) it helps us keep a record of the initial conversations with all educators, and 2) it is a document that everyone can look at to see if educators in other groups came up with a similar topic. I always encourage educators to seek out other educators that are looking to tackle the same kind of Professionally Driven journey in order to build collaboration. Notice, however, that these groups are formed naturally. They are not designated by me or the administrator. This builds the idea of sustainable autonomy. If a group of educators on a specific topic becomes too large, I recommend dividing the group into two smaller groups. However, those two groups can collaborate whenever needed.

How you choose the groups is also important. In most cases, I leave it up to the instructional coaches to do the groupings but usually say to them, "Put any educators who you feel are more 'vocal' or fixed mindset with me if you want. That includes administrators, too." I don't offer this because I feel I am "the best" at coaxing fixed mindset people or think highly of myself. I do it because I'm not in the building on a daily basis, and it may be easier for me to ask different kinds of questions to prompt deeper thinking for some of those educators. Also, we don't have any prior history that could possibly stir up negative emotions or resentment while having such personal reflection about weaknesses in the instruction. My neutrality in this situation could help the educator focus more on ineffective instructional strategies and not them, the instructor.

On Kick-Off Day
We may have, for example, 10 groups of 10 educators each. If I am the lead facilitator in my group, we go around the circle and each educator expresses what they think their topic could be. For each educator, the rest of the group checks to make sure that the three

filters for an appropriate topic are met. If the topic checks out, that topic is recorded in the Google Doc, and we move on to the next educator. We continue this until we have gone around the entire circle.

If we come to an educator that is struggling to identify a topic based on a weak spot in their instruction, then conversation from the entire group is welcome in order to help that educator identify a topic. Usually I will start this conversation with the question, "Where do you see your students continually operating in the lowest levels of Bloom's taxonomy?" This question can be tricky for some, because I am not inviting the other educators in the circle to point out that educator's instructional weaknesses. However, I am inviting the other educators to use their own examples as a possible place for that educator to start. As soon as you have educators calling out each other's weaknesses, you will find yourself in a group of educators who quickly become extremely defensive about their teaching. No one is a perfect educator, and if they are of a fixed mindset, it is difficult for them to even admit that there is a weakness. But if you have other educators claiming they have weaknesses, then it is easier for a fixed mindset educator to admit that they may also have a weakness in their own instruction.

It is important to note that no educators leave the group until all have identified an appropriate topic for their first Professionally Driven journey. Even though this may sound small, I feel it's this "no educator left behind" mentality that begins to build that culture of learning together. As we know, all learning is social. Therefore, we should encourage educators to support one another in all phases of the learning process. If there is an educator who is really struggling to hone in on their topic, and it is holding time back for the rest of the group to begin their journey, then I will volunteer to sit back and work with that educator one-on-one. This doesn't happen often, but the educator just needs to have further conversation and sometimes, a one-on-one conversation doesn't escalate anxiety as much as a conversation with the whole group. This is also why I recommend those lead facilitators be an instructional coach or a consultant of some kind who can sense this kind of anxiety and work to de-escalate it. We want the Professionally Driven journey to feel like a model for open dialogue and communication between all. Open communication leads to impactful collaboration.

TIGHT VS. LOOSE IMPLEMENTATION OF THE MODEL

To sum up the nuts and bolts of this model, it may be easiest to provide a simple table to illustrate what parts of this model should be treated tighter (more rigid in their implementation) vs. what should be treated more loosely (school districts have more leniency to decide what works best for their district). If an item in the *Tight* column can also have qualities that are *Loose*, then you find those qualities in the *Loose* column. However, if the box in the *Loose* column is blank, that means the item in the *Tight* column is non-negotiable in order to assure the best chance possible for supporting the *Big Three to be PD*: growth mindset, intrinsic motivation, sustainable autonomy.

TIME

Tight	Loose
Offer personalized PD time a minimum of two hours/month.	Offering it more frequently would make the time between training and learning feel more balanced.
Conduct the recognition ceremony at minimum on a quarterly basis.	The recognition ceremony could be offered more frequently as educators progress from one phase to the next.
Provide time at the beginning of a personalized PD session for any that would like to deliver their reflection talk.	
Shift to the Professionally Driven model gradually by introducing it in three separate sessions: The Teaser, The Reveal, The Kick-Off.	How far apart these sessions take place can vary depending on your existing professional development schedule.
Keep personalized PD time sacred. DO NOT cut into personalized PD time with staff meetings or anything else that takes time away from the process of learning.	
DO NOT put a time limit on a journey. Do not say to an educator, "You have until ____ to finish your Research phase." Some educators play the "wait game", because they've been conditioned to do so. They need to see this is a holistic learning process before they are willing to commit the time and energy.	

PLACE

Tight	Loose
Always meet in the same location at the beginning of every personalized PD session.	If your district has multiple buildings, you may need to designate an initial meeting place just within your building.
Try to have the Tech Sessions in the same room/space every time.	
Use the same designated work areas/classrooms for every personalized PD session.	If an educator, or small group of educators, need to meet in a space that is not in a designated work area, be sure to let an instructional coach know so they can plan to support them in a timely manner. However, I would not recommend doing this frequently. Only in special circumstances.

LOGISTICS

Tight	Loose
Do not leave out any of the four phases: Research, Integrate, Reflect, Share.	
Administrators should go on their own learning journeys, too.	
Treat the whole process as one of communication and learning, NOT evaluation.	
Use a "central hub" to house all Professionally Driven information/materials.	What you use as your "central hub" is up to the district.
Use a local/personalized analogy that illustrates the four phases.	The analogy can be tied to anything that resonates with your district.
Use recognition pieces that educators would be proud to put on display.	Most choose to tie the recognition to the analogy, but it's not required.
Each journey MUST be centered on **positive effects on learner outcomes.**	

QUESTIONS TO CONSIDER WHEN IMPLEMENTING THE PROFESSIONALLY DRIVEN MODEL...

- What is the current time frame of your contractual PD time? Is it weekly? Is it consistent?
- What will your analogy be?
- What will the recognition pieces be? Will they be tied to your analogy in some way?
- Where will be your initial meeting location at the beginning of every personalized PD session? Where will the designated work areas be?
- How will you allot time for the Reflection phase?
- Where will Tech Sessions be held?

Chapter 6
The Coaching Role

In any journey worth taking, it is rarely taken alone.

Up to this point, I have laid out the **Why** and **How** of empowering all adult learners to become Professionally Driven. However, there is a key person (or persons, in some districts) in this whole process that plays a major role: the instructional coach. Instructional coaches are integral members to both the Why and the How. I have focused on educators' (including administrators) roles in the process; however, all the aspects of the Professionally Driven model that the coach is involved in are focused on in this chapter so that it can be easily referenced if necessary.

This doesn't mean if you're *not* an instructional coach, you should just skip this chapter. Understanding everyone's role in the Professionally Driven journey is important. If you're a teacher or an administrator, you need to understand what the coach's role is so you leverage the kind of support they can provide while you embark on your Professionally Driven journey.

Coaching Guide Questions

The term **coach** actually derives from the word *stagecoach* that was first used in the 15th century when a coach was pulled by horses to get passengers from one place to another. Over the course of time, the word coach was used in education before it was used in athletics; today, we associate it more with athletics. The reason for adopting the word in these areas is the idea of a person who is helping to get someone else from one place to the next, one goal to the next, or to another area of learning. So a coach, in this sense, truly is a needed part of any journey.

An *instructional coach* then is someone who assists with an instructional journey of improvement. This can vary from district to district, building to building, or even person to person. For the most part, an instructional coach is the one who assists in improving an educator's instructional practice through a multitude of strategies.

You can use whatever coaching model you wish, but what they all have in common is the importance of asking questions for reflection.

A question that I often get, and one that came up in that initial planning session at Oelwein was, *How will we know when an educator is ready for the next phase?* This is, perhaps, the single greatest role a coach plays in this entire model. Like the original stagecoach, your role to is to help educators get to the next phase on their journey.

I'm not saying a coach is the gatekeeper with the rubber stamp that gives the final approval on whether or not an educator moves to the next phase. The coach is simply that soundboard that asks the necessary questions and makes sure all the prerequisite thinking has taken place before moving on. The coach is like a verbal mirror. They intentionally listen and interpret what they hear so the educator can understand if what they're thinking is clear or not. It is advantageous for both the educator and the coach to be purposeful in thinking through the next steps of each phase. That is why we also developed the **Coaching Guide Questions**.

The Coaching Guide Questions were created in partnership by the original instructional coaches at the Oelwein School District: Jill Kelly (@teacherjkelly), Kristi Truvenga (@kdmvenga), and Lori Decker. They had taken some instructional coaching trainings and came away wanting to develop a systematic way for coaches to engage in meaningful conversations with educators. The goal was to create a simple list of the most pertinent questions that could lend themselves to an *informal conversation* between instructional coach and adult learner. They are *not* meant to be treated as hoops to jump through.

If a learner feels they are ready for the next phase in their learning journey, all we ask is that they set up a time to have a conversation with a coach. This could be during personalized PD times. Below are the questions used to guide those conversations after each phase feels complete. You may see some questions that need rewording based on your district's or even your state's needs, but the focus is on the big ideas being posed in each phase that serve to ensure success when moving onto the next phase. Those are indicated with bold font.

RESEARCH PHASE COACHING GUIDE QUESTIONS

1. What is your topic for research?
2. What prior knowledge do you have on this topic?
3. How/Where does this fit into your curriculum?
4. Which Teaching Standards/I Can statements align with this topic?
5. What resource mediums were used in your research? List them all and include links if you wish.
6. How will this be effective in your classroom?
7. **How will this topic enhance and support student learning? How will you apply this strategy?**
8. **How will this strategy allow you to do classroom instruction differently?**
9. **How will you adapt this to meet all student needs?**
10. What other resources will you need to integrate this in your classroom?
11. How do you expect the students to understand and utilize any new technology that may be involved? When will you teach them?
12. What are your outcome goals?
13. Within your topic area, how will your instructional strategies and combined technology support student-centered learning?
14. **In the next phase, what will you look for that tells you it's working?**

INTEGRATION PHASE COACHING GUIDE QUESTIONS

1. What steps did you take in ensuring successful integration?
2. What resources/technologies did you use in your classroom from your research?
3. Describe the content and/or process topic(s) for the lesson(s).
4. **Describe the student learning goals/objectives addressed in the lesson. What do you want them to walk away with?**
5. Describe your students (e.g. grade level, and specific learning needs/preferences).
6. Walk me through the lesson/project as it unfolded in the classroom.
7. What educational technologies (digital and non-digital) did you use and how did you and your students use them?

8. Describe any contextual information (e.g. access to a computer lab, materials and resources available or particular departmental/school-wide initiatives) that influenced the design or implementation of the lesson/project.
9. How did you assess this activity/project/strategy?
10. **What evidence did you collect to identify success?**
11. **What worked? What didn't work?**
12. **What changes have you seen with how you teach?**
13. **What changes have you seen in how your students are learning?**

REFLECTION PHASE COACHING GUIDE QUESTIONS

1. What steps did you take?
2. How do you think the strategy is working overall?
3. What went well? What didn't go well?
4. **What happened in this class that cognitively engaged students?**
5. What comparisons might you make between the lesson you planned/envisioned and the one you taught?
6. What formative assessment data did you gather from the students to let you know how the lesson/unit went? What did you do with this data to change the level of integration?
7. **What moments of personal enlightenment did you notice?**
8. **What teaching standards did you meet in the process?**

SHARING PHASE COACHING GUIDE QUESTIONS

This particular section doesn't require any Coaching Guide Questions. However, the instructional coach may need to support the educator in creating the necessary accounts or preparing the presentation to be made. In general, the coach must support the educator as they create their method to share their journey outside their district. A lot of the critical thinking for this phase was already done in the Reflection phase.

CONVERSATIONS MATTER MOST

In one of the schools that I worked with, we were in the early stages of implementing this model. Educators were filling out the Coaching Guide Questions in a document and answering each question by typing their answers. When educators decided to write out the answers was up to them. Some educators preferred to do this ahead of time, which was completely fine. However, when I spoke with one educator, he expressed that typing out the answers to these questions felt like another hoop to jump through. I can see how an educator may feel that way. If I were the instructional coach in this situation, I don't think typing out the answers is the most important part. I think as long as an educator has reflected on the questions in this process, and they can intelligently articulate their answers in our face-to-face conversation, that would suffice. However, in a larger school district where it might be difficult to arrange face-to-face time, I can see how typing out the answers so the coach can read it at another time might be beneficial.

Typing out the answers for a coach to read later and give feedback should *not* replace a face-to-face conversation. It's important to explore as many of the questions as possible but doing so in a non-procedural way. I have discovered that when an educator moves too quickly from one phase to the next without doing the proper reflection and planning, they usually end up back at the previous phase. For example, if an educator treats this whole process as a "have-to" and wishes to just move on to the Integration phase, more than likely they will end up back at the Research phase because they didn't properly reflect and think through the process. They won't end up back there because someone told them they had to; they just realize they can't successfully move forward.

I recall one such classroom teacher who saw this whole process as something to quickly get over with. He claimed he was done with his research and was ready for the Integration phase in a matter of just days. My coaching senses were tingling with skepticism, but I decided to meet with him to go through the *Research Phase Coaching Guide Questions*. I didn't want the conversation to feel formal, so I didn't go with the Q1:A1 format. Instead, I simply asked about his topic, what weak spot he thought he could turn into a strength by tackling the topic, and so on—just some of the big idea questions from the Research phase. It didn't take long for me to hear that he was treating all of this as a "have-to."

He couldn't articulate very well his thinking or what new knowledge he gained from the Research phase. However, all I did was ask questions for clarification, and repeat back or interpret what I heard so he could hear his thoughts out loud. He was adamant that he knew what he needed to do for the next phase. I had a hunch that it wasn't going to go the way he was thinking, because he couldn't clearly express to me what he felt successful integration looked like, or what he was going to look for in order to determine if it was successful. But I'm not the gatekeeper with the rubber stamp. I don't get to say, "You shall not pass." All I said to him was, "I can see you're energized about this and wanting to really integrate it. Ultimately, the call is yours, but I would encourage you to think about what information you will be looking for to determine if it's successful or not. Can you make me a deal, though?"

"What's that?" he replied.

"If you get stuck or need some help, be sure to reach out to me?"

"Yep. Will do," he said hurriedly.

A few weeks later, this teacher reached back out to me after he felt frustrated with the Integration phase. He didn't know why he wasn't getting the results he was looking for. After some conversation, he realized he needed to go back and do some more research.

Now, I could have told him that was more than likely going to happen and prevented him from moving on to the next phase. Instead, I gave him the autonomy to self-discover so he would be more inclined to go deeper with his research the next time. As an instructional coach, you have to be the person that makes it OK to fail forward. If all educators (administrators *and* teachers) are embarking on learning journeys, the coach is the support, and in this non-evaluative role, you can do so in a very non-threatening way.

Also, where we get a true shift in teaching and thinking is through the conversations we have with others. These *Coaching Guide Questions* should not serve as a device for accountability, but rather as a device to help guide meaningful conversations about instruction.

THE CHECKLISTS

Some people really like checklists. They receive that self-satisfactory feeling of accomplishment when an item gets crossed off. For some, checklists help to stay focused on the task at hand, and more importantly, it may help them understand where they are with their process:

- "I'm halfway done with my project."
- "I still have several steps to go."
- "One more, and I'm finished."

Checklists can help breakdown any larger project or process into more digestible and achievable chunks.

With each phase, we included checklists for those Type-A educators who would like that kind of guidance. I realize that using checklists gives the impression of top-down mentality or accountability. It might seem like we'll provide the hoops, you just need to jump through them. But that's not the case.

The checklist is nothing more than that: a checklist. It's used at each phase to help the educator understand if they have completed the suggested steps in that particular phase. *These are merely for the educator's reference.* The coach does not have these on a clipboard to check off each one as if to provide an inspection for completeness. In fact, the coach doesn't use them, unless there is someone who is really looking for that guidance. So the checklists may not even be used by all educators, only those that are hesitant in determining the direction of their path. As I mentioned in prior chapters, these are usually the educators who are afraid to be considered "non-compliant" and simply wish to know if they are heading in the right direction. Don't mistake this for the professional development creators laying out the path for the educators. It's a tool for the educator to self-assess if they are ready for the next phase or not.

I've sat down with many educators who become anxious in deciding if they are ready for the next phase: a decision that no coach should ever make for them. But if they come to me questioning if they are ready or not, I will sometimes use the Checklist for that phase as a tool to help them make that decision for themselves. Whether the coach goes through the Checklist with them or simply directs them to it is the call of the coach. I would think this depends on the educator and their relationship with them. But keep in mind that the goal is for every educator to feel empowered to become Professionally Driven and be able to make decisions for themselves.

It should not feel like educators are being led by the hand down a path determined for them.

The following Checklists were once again developed in partnership with the original instructional coaches at the Oelwein School District. They are recommended, but like the Coaching Guide Questions, may need slight tweaking based on district or state needs.

RESEARCH PHASE CHECKLIST
- Decide on a topic to research.
- Document 4-6 (just a suggestion) research resources using a variety of mediums.
- Visit with your instructional/tech coach for support.
- Put any findings and resources in your Professionally Driven Google folder.
- Meet with your instructional coach and go through the Coaching Guide Questions.

INTEGRATION PHASE CHECKLIST
- Integrate your research into a lesson or unit.
- Visit with your instructional coach for support.
- Collect evidence that tells you if the strategy is working or not.
- Review evidence/data and tweak as necessary until you feel it's working with fidelity.
- Meet with your instructional coach and go through the Coaching Guide Questions.

REFLECTION PHASE CHECKLIST
- Decide how you wish to share your process of turning your weak spot into a strength (video, TED Talk, etc.)
- Visit with your instructional coach for support in ensuring your entire journey is included.
- Present your journey within your district.
- Meet with your instructional coach and go through the Coaching Guide Questions.

Note: If the educator chooses to do a TED-style talk, encourage the educator to have it recorded so it can be viewed later by others. It will be helpful if they wish to review it before possibly presenting at a conference. Or if you are in a larger district, the recorded presentation can easily be shared with other buildings in the district.

SHARING PHASE CHECKLIST

The Sharing Phase Checklist is going to vary depending on what method they wish to use to *share outside the district*. If an educator wishes to present at a conference or blog about their journey in a few different blog posts, the checklist will need to be tailored for the educator. A coach can assist in doing this. Developing a single universal checklist for everyone would not be possible. If a checklist is wanted in this phase, it will need to created by the educator and coach.

SUPPORTING THE PROCESS

The Professionally Driven model relies on some kind of instructional coach or teacher-leader to support educators through their journey. Just like Luke Skywalker needed Yoda in *Star Wars* and Odysseus needed Athena in *The Odyssey*, educators will need support and guidance on their Professionally Driven journey. In any journey worth taking, it is rarely taken alone, and the kind of support a coach provides can vary.

Some states have an outside support system that serves in this role of instructional coach, like an education agency of some kind. Some districts are hiring these instructional coaching positions to remain in-house. I've even worked with a couple of districts that started this model without the coaching role. In this case, I would recommend the responsibilities in this chapter be divvied up in some fashion to ensure that all parts of the model are supported.

When instructional coaches are in place, it provides the extra support that educators need when they become stuck on their Professionally Driven journeys. Educators must know that they have the support they need when they need it, otherwise it becomes very difficult for educators (like students) to stay motivated on their journey. In order to better support educators on their Professionally Driven journeys, the role and function of the coach at each phase needs to be clear.

It is best to describe the coach's role by breaking up the time in three types: **time prior**, **time during**, and **time outside** the personalized

PD sessions. Again, the personalized PD sessions that we are talking about are those days that have been specified on the professional development calendar for work on the Professionally Driven journeys. These should be, at minimum, once a month (reference back to the previous chapter if needed).

TIME PRIOR

Prior to a personalized PD session, an educator who feels he or she is ready to move on to the next phase needs to contact their coach. This could be something as simple as an email, stopping them in the hall, or even setting up a Google Form to request a coaching session. The coach then knows to make an attempt to meet with that educator during the personalized PD time.

A key component of the personalized PD time is the recognition of educators on their journey. Coaches can also organize everything that may be needed for a Recognition Ceremony prior to a day where personalized PD time is scheduled. If the personalized PD time is scheduled for a Friday, for example, I would start organizing what's needed that Monday before.

- Double check with educators to see who is ready to be recognized.
- Organize the recognition pieces that will be needed.
- Prepare the slideshow if one is being used (educator's name, phase, and topic)
- If there is any kind of music, have it ready to go.
- See if there are any educators wanting to present their Reflection phase.

I recommend the coach be the organizer of this for one big reason: this process is supposed to feel as non-evaluative as possible, and the coach is not the evaluator. Remember, I encourage all teachers and administrators to embark on a journey. The coach is then the person who really knows where all educators are on their journey.

TIME DURING

Educators and coaches need time to be able to discuss their journey. This time needs to be valued and offered at every personalized PD session. Once an instructional coach and educator have time to sit down and meet during the personalized PD time, they have the opportunity to work through the Coaching Guide Questions and/or Checklists where the educator determines if he or she is ready to move on to the next phase. When coach and the educator are done having the necessary conversation, the coach can easily find the next educator that requested to meet.

If there are no Coaching Session requests for that particular personalized PD time, then I encourage the coach to simply check in with educators they think may need support. I would try and check in with educators that would benefit from a conversation, more for my sake to simply catch up on their journey. Being willing to have open conversations is essential to growth in a Professionally Driven journey.

A great coach is just like a great educator: they know when to ask the right questions in order to prompt more thinking. Even though the Coaching Guide Questions are put in place and used, it doesn't mean the coach can't ask other informal questions. As I mentioned earlier, a coach is a soundboard for the educator. Their purpose is to listen intently to the process and thinking that the educator is going through and ask more questions to prompt more thinking.

This same method of probing with questions holds true for even those educators who are more reluctant to begin their Professionally Driven journey. If I have not received a request to meet with a certain educator for a while, I might use some of the personalized PD time to meet with that educator and simply ask:

- "How's it going with your journey?"
- "What support do you need from me?"
- "What resources have you collected that you found to be the most valuable so far?"
- "What resources do you feel you still need?"

Of course, I would do my best to make sure that I am using an approach that seems more conversational and cooperative instead of evaluative, as if I were looking over their shoulder to see if they are working on something.

On days where a small portion of the personalized PD time is spent recognizing educators as professionals for their work in moving from one phase to the next, it should be the coach to recognize each educator accordingly. They should be the one to hand out the recognition pieces, too. While the Recognition Ceremony could ultimately be prepared by the coach, the coach must work with any other professional development team members (most likely administrators) to ensure the personalized PD time is protected and a culture of learning is continually supported.

TIME OUTSIDE

Since time to work on a Professionally Driven journey only occurs monthly (though it could be more frequently), where does that leave the coach on days that aren't designated personalized PD time? First of all, I would argue that *every day* is a day for personalized PD time. But on the days that educators don't get the time blocked off by the district to focus on their Professionally Driven journey, what role do the coaches serve? This is probably going to be different depending on the district and what coaching cycle or method they choose to support and implement. However, the Professionally Driven model can be included in this continual support as well.

Besides the *Coaching Guide Questions* and the *Checklists*, a coach can be helpful in every phase of the journey, but how exactly they are utilized will depend on each phase.

Research Phase

When an educator is able to identify the journey they will embark on, they may have a difficult time knowing where to go to seek more information along the way. The coach is a great place to start. If it is a topic that the coach may not have that much knowledge of, then it is up to the coach to point educators in the right direction of where they can find more information. Additional resources can include blogs, videos, books, and even connections with other educators through some kind of professional learning network (PLN). The coach is the bridge to more information for educators in the Research phase.

Also in the Research phase, educators can become easily diverted from their original focus. It is important for coaches to help educators stay focused on what will have a positive impact on learner outcomes, which could include learning standards. But these learning standards shouldn't be used to pull an educator in one direction or another based on what the coach thinks they should do. It's their journey, but a coach can help prevent educators from straying off and finding a new topic that is the latest and greatest thing, especially when it may not have a direct positive effect on learner outcomes.

Integration Phase

When an educator is ready to begin integrating their new teaching strategy, a coach can help them develop and organize a plan to begin integrating the strategy effectively.

The big question being addressed during the Integration Phase is, "What will you collect to help you determine if this strategy is working or not?" A coach can help the educator determine what methods to use to collect formative assessment data, as well as help them work through that data to determine if retooling is necessary. This may look like a trial-and-error process for the educator, and a coach can help them refine the strategy until the educator feels successful.

Reflection Phase

During the Reflection Phase, the educator is reflecting back on their journey and the process, not necessarily the final product. The educator can do this any way they wish as long as they are sharing their journey from instructional weakness to strength within the district. The coach then is the support the educator may need in order to plan their presentation. The coach is there to discuss out loud with the educator the questions in the *Coaching Guide* that can lead to deeper reflection for the educator.

The coach may assist the educator in preparing this reflection no matter what type of delivery format. If the educator chooses a TED-style talk, the coach might assist by helping them organize their presentation or assist them with using a new presentation tool. If an educator decides to create a video to be shared with the staff, the coach might assist by filming classroom activities or help with editing tools. Regardless of how the reflection is delivered, the coach is the soundboard to make sure the reflection is deep and not superficial.

Sharing Phase

In the sharing phase, educators are required to share their new understanding outside the district. Two common ways to do this is to either present at a conference or blog about the journey and share it via social media, although other methods are also acceptable. In a case where an educator decides to present their new knowledge at a conference, the coach may assist the educator in organizing their presentation and using the appropriate tool for delivery. A coach may also look for conferences in which the educator could apply to present. However, if an educator would rather blog about their experience and share it via social media, the coach may help the educator decide which blogging platform to use, how to create an account, and how to organize their blog post. The coach is also the one to encourage the educator to share their new understanding via social media. This could require getting the educator set up with an account and choose the appropriate channels to share their post. This encourages the educator to build their PLN (Professional Learning Network) and to contribute to that community of educators.

KEEPING THE LEARNING ORGANIZED

In my first year of implementing the Professionally Driven model, it quickly became apparent that it was going to be difficult to keep track of where educators were on their learning journeys. It was like a patient who was being seen by multiple doctors, or maybe even one doctor trying to keep track of multiple patients. In either case, we needed to create a system that helped organize and document all of this learning. The documenting part isn't to "prove" that the educators have gone through the process, but rather to help other educators who may be interested in going on a similar journey. For coaches, documenting is to help keep track of conversations of where educators are on their journeys. Being able to search it all for easy communication and sharing was critical early in our implementation.

We had already established a central hub for all of the educators to access the necessary documents and questions (Chp. 5 - The Model), but we needed a place for educators to store their learning. For this purpose, we used Google Drive. Doing so allowed us to accomplish two things:

1. It allowed educators to store many of their necessary materials in a single place, helping them stay organized from one phase to the next.
2. It allows all educators to easily share their learning with other educators in the district. When educators do this, it will continually strengthen the culture of communication and sharing within your district.

Most schools I currently work with already have a Google domain. Other schools may be using Office 365 or another similar education domain. In most cases, you are able to create a file sharing system that is similar to the described below:

1. The Tech Coordinator creates a generic school Google account, one that can be accessed by any person that may need to access it. If a person within your district creates this folder with their school account, and they should happen to leave or retire, they risk losing the folder for the entire district.
2. Create a folder called [*your school district*] *Professionally Driven Journeys.* Make this folder searchable by the entire district.
3. Within that folder, create a folder for each level or for each building (i.e. Elementary, Middle School, High School)
4. In each of the respective folders, have educators either create their own or create one for them ahead of time.
5. As each educator embarks on their learning journeys, it's recommended that they create folders within their own personal folder that are each labeled with the journey title.
6. In each journey, they may want to create a folder for each phase (Research, Integration, Reflect, Share).
7. Then, whatever they wish to put in those folders is up to them and their coach, but I would recommend at minimum putting in the *Coaching Guide Question* and/or *Checklists.*

The following chart visually illustrates the steps above:

This is just one method to help keep all of the learning within your district organized and searchable. However, you may find another method that better suits your district's needs or the needs of individual educators. I had one classroom teacher approach me and said, "I'm not doing those Google folders."

Taken back a little I asked back, "Well, do you use some other way to organize your learning?

He thought for a quick second. "Will a 3-ring binder work?"

I prevented myself from chuckling slightly and encouragingly replied, "Sure. Whatever helps you on your journey. Let's give the 3-ring binder a go this time, but we'll find something else that can be more easily shared with others in the whole district."

Whether it is the highly searchable and shareable route that uses some kind of technology or the more analogue route of a 3-ring binder, I would have the organization method be tied in with the central hub for your district's Professionally Driven journey. Have the folder linked somewhere. This will cut down on a lot of confusion for both coaches and the educators that they serve in this Professionally Driven model.

QUESTIONS TO CONSIDER FOR THE COACHING ROLE IN THE PROFESSIONALLY DRIVEN MODEL...

- How will the educators in your district get in touch with you to set up a Coaching Session?
- How will you set up and organize the Recognition Ceremony?
- How will you help keep the lines of communication clear and welcoming?
- How will your district keep the learning organized?
- How will you remain in a cooperative role and not an evaluative one?
- What time do you plan to use to support educators in all the phases of this Professionally Driven model?
- How will the personalized PD time be protected and kept sacred?

Professionally Driven Educator
Jill Kelly
Instructional Coach

As an instructional coach at Oelwein Middle School, Jill plays a key role in helping educators progress on their journey. She also has to help them find their right path to start on. Hear Jill's story in her own words as she describes working with varying educators on their journeys and helping them realize it's not about the tech.

While working on an action research project for my master's degree, I realized how beneficial that process was for an educator's growth. Recently, I transitioned from my position as the district's talented and gifted coordinator to an instructional technology coach. In this new position, I wondered how I could guide our 6th-12th grade educators through their own action research projects based on the instructional and technology needs in their classrooms. During my first year as an instructional technology coach, our district was going 1:1 with MacBook Air computers, and my focus in this position was, "How can I help educators integrate technology in their classrooms?" My goals were to motivate and encourage educators to move toward creating student-centered, project-based learning environments where technology was seamlessly integrated into the process.

In preparation for the school year, my district offered technology professional development once a month during the prior year. Each month, five or six sessions were offered and educators could choose the session(s) that fit their needs. This type of tech PD continued through the fall of the school year. Data from staff feedback surveys began to reveal that some educators needed more information and time to integrate these tools into their curriculum. The district technology committee met to discuss how to meet the tech PD needs of our educators. During this meeting, I brought up the idea of PD gamification, which was gaining popularity.

Our superintendent invited Jarod Bormann, a technology integrationist from our AEA (area education agency), to help us work on designing a more personalized PD for our 6th-12th grade educators. During our first meeting, a few of us shared examples of personalized tech PD that had been gamified. Jarod pointed out that in each example the technology was being taught in isolation. We discussed the need to guide our educators toward using technology to transform their teaching. One purpose of the 1:1 rollout was to motivate and encourage educators to use the technology to move toward creating student-centered, relevant, and rigorous learning environments where technology is seamlessly integrated into the process. The ultimate goal of Jarod's was to create transformative learning experiences that would lead to high levels of student learning.

Jarod came back a week later and had incorporated our gamification ideas with a model that would ask educators to choose something in their classroom that they would like to change or add to impact student outcome in a positive way. Since this would be considered "technology PD," educators were asked to include technology in some way, but to focus on intended student outcomes. The plan was based on the phases of Jarod's Professionally Driven PD model.

Each phase would have a checklist of tasks to complete and a tech coach that would meet with educators and have a discussion of the journey. I worked with the high school instructional coaches to develop those two pieces for this phase. At that moment, I realized that this technology PD was going to take our educators informally through the action research steps of a master's degree program in order to enhance student outcomes. I literally stood up in front of the other instructional coach and exclaimed, "This is amazing!" I was thrilled that I could contribute questions that would make the educators think about their teaching and student outcomes.

When our district rolled out the new technology PD with gamification features to our educators, the instructional coaches were there to support the process. Some educators were excited to have time to work on new teaching ideas they wanted to try, while others were not as excited. They were not used to having time and freedom to work on their own classroom needs. It was vital for these educators to have the support of an instructional coach. In order to create a safe, authentic learning environment, they needed to work with a non-judgmental partner. Whether real or imagined, when administrators fill this role, their presence tends to bring with it a sense of judgement that can mar the process.

To support our goals, I made myself available to educators during their planning time. I found many were having a hard time coming up with project ideas, hence something like the first step in the action research process: defining a topic. During these conversations, they kept focusing on the technology instead of first focusing on the instructional goal. The educator's mindset was that this project was solely about the technology and not about the content they were teaching and the approach they were using to teach the content.

I began asking them to forget about the technology and think about what they wanted their students to learn in their class. *What was their instructional goal?* Over and over, the response to this question would be accompanied with a look of revelation; I could actually see light bulbs going on. They started to move beyond focusing on only the technology and started thinking about the student outcomes they wanted to achieve as a result of their instruction. This change of focus helped them move toward making changes to their teaching pedagogy, instead of focusing on what technology they thought they had to use.

The Professionally Driven model allowed me, as an instructional coach, to work with educators in authentic ways on meaningful and deep pedagogical and instructional transformations. Through the coaching and questioning process, educators were able to identify meaningful individualized projects that would impact student learning. The partnership between the educator and the instructional coach gives the educator support and feedback so the project succeeds. The PD time during the year was also vital. It gave the educator and instructional coach time to go through the process and build trusting relationships.

One of the most inspiring moments in this journey came from my conversation with a building principal, Mary Beth (her vignette appeared earlier in the book). I was motivated by this conversation and by numerous other conversations with educators in our district to continue to focus on holding conversations and building relationships. Shortly after the conversation with Mary Beth, I was working the 5th-8th grade band educator and focusing her project on teaching the students how to effectively practice. During our conversations she continued to get stuck with the system that was in place. Our district had purchased an expensive site license of interactive music software for student practice and she felt obligated to use it. I asked her to put the district money aside and tell me in a perfect world what she envisioned for the students.

It was like a switch came on. She immediately explained to me that she didn't think the 5th and 6th grade students used the music practice software to its full potential because they didn't know how to effectively practice. She wanted to design a process to break down practice and teach students each part individually. From our conversation, I asked if the district could start the practice software when students were in 7th grade? We approached the other band educators and administration, all were in support of her plan. She developed a website that students could use at home to learn each step of a good practice session. She included video clips, logs, and parent information guides to support students through this learning process. The coaching conversation gave her the arena to explore all possibilities and trusted her professional judgement to decide what was best for her students.

Instructional coaches are key to a successful Professionally Driven model, they support educators in making connections in their own classrooms between the content they teach, how they teach, and what technology will be used to impact student learning and outcomes.

CHAPTER 7
CLIMB THE MOUNTAIN

It's not how many mountains you conquer;
it's how many times you conquer the mountain.

In Glacier National Park in Montana, in the Lewis Range of mountains, there stands a stoic snowy peak that looks over the McDonald Creek Valley. Before 1901, this mountain was known as Goat Mountain. I can only assume it was called that because of the mountain goats that can be found grazing in the area. Also prior to that year, not a single person had ever ascended the full 8,952 feet of Goat Mountain where the summit lies. However, in 1901, a man and his wife decided to spend their honeymoon not lying on a beach or someplace tropical and warm. They decided to celebrate their nuptials by spending their first days as husband and wife completing an adventure that no one else had: climb Goat Mountain. They were not mountaineers by trade; one was a well-known author and the other a leading physiologist at Harvard. But because of their journey in reaching the summit on July 19th of 1901, the mountain was later renamed after the couple: Mount Cannon. Does the name Cannon sound familiar? No?

Walter Cannon was the American physiologist who coined the phrase *fight-or-flight*, mentioned in Chapter 2. I find it uncanny that the man who studied and labeled the physiological response that stands as the ultimate fork in the road in our venture towards grit, perseverance, and eventually a growth mindset, is also the same man who chose to *Fight*.

When I think of someone whom I would consider **driven**, I think of mountaineers. I have never scaled a full mountain, myself, but I admire Dr. Cannon and his wife and any others who look up at a summit and say, "I wonder what it's like to stand up there?" What a feeling that must be to stand at Point A, then be able to physically see with your own eyes and point your finger at Point B. Then to reflect on all it would take to get *there*. To literally see the snow, sharp inclines, and chiseled rocks and understand how arduous the journey will be...and willingly take the first step anyway. That's being *driven*. That's fully understanding how physically and mentally taxing it will be, but knowing the view from the summit will be worth it. It's realizing that who you are at Point A will not be the same person that reaches Point B, and that thought energizes the first step and may very well energize the last one that needs to be taken.

Maybe you, yourself, are a mountaineer, or maybe you have the privilege of knowing someone who is. I do not. But I have watched a number of documentaries on mountain climbing. In almost every one of them, when the climbers finally reach the top, they comment on the view or a new profound sense of self. This reminds me of a quote from David McCullough, Jr.'s commencement speech at Wellesley High School that went on to be a viral YouTube video and later spurred his book called, *You Are Not Special*. "Don't climb the mountain so the world can see *you*. Climb the mountain so you can see the *world*." It's this juxtaposition in perspective that reveals the intent of those that are truly driven for a grander purpose: to gain a new understanding.

The most important task in beginning your Professionally Driven journey is identifying your mountain. We have identified Point B as the summit: a positive effect on learner outcomes. Point A then could be an infinite number of starting places at the base of the mountain. However, it helps to have an idea of how to decide which spot is the best place to start. By asking ourselves where we see students continually operating in the lowest levels of Bloom's Taxonomy, we narrow down our options. Then, taking those options through the three filters mentioned in Chapter 2, we hopefully discover the spot (the weak spot) where we should begin our journey. And because the educator is the one that determined the starting point, they are far more inclined to be willing to take that first brave step.

As they reach each camp on their Professionally Driven mountain, they get to plant their flag and be recognized in the progression. They also have a chance to reflect, regather, and devote some time to planning for the next phase with their guide, the instructional coach. The Reflection phase is my personal favorite. It's that point where a climber is three-fourths of the way up the mountain. The summit looks so close, but it's that moment where they get the opportunity to look back down the mountain and realize how far they've come, knowing full well that the journey is not yet complete. And when they eventually conquer the summit, they have now gained a new understanding, or maybe even a new sense of self. They have experienced a change in educational beliefs. The educator that stands at the summit is no longer the educator that stood at the foot of the mountain.

So what happens after an educator has reached the pinnacle? Do they go find another mountain to conquer? No. They look for another path to reach the summit.

Remember, the summit is **a positive effect on learner outcomes**. This can be the same summit no matter the grade-level or content area. So imagine you see a mountain. This mountain is only open for you to climb, unless you invite others to trek on a similar journey with you. But once you reach the summit, you start back at the bottom and ascend once again, trying to find another way to have a positive effect on learner outcomes. I would be willing to bet that your second journey will not have the same starting point, nor will you take the exact same route, but you will reach the four different camps (phases) every time. If you continually ascend to the summit of *positive effects on learner outcomes* over the course of your entire career as an educator, think of all the learning and growing that you will do. Think of the great benefits your learners will reap from it, and I say this to teachers *and* administrators. This, to me, sounds like a Professionally Driven educator.

So, to put my own juxtaposition in perspective: It's not how many mountains you conquer; it's how many times you can conquer the mountain. Does it sound crazy to encourage someone to climb the same mountain over and over again?

Apa Sherpa and Phurba Tashi are two of the most respected climbers in the world. Sherpa, a Nepalese native who currently resides in Utah, and Tashi, a climber featured in the 2009 Discovery Channel series *Everest: Beyond the Limit*, currently share the world record for most ascents up Mt. Everest. Since 1990, these two men have stood at the top of the tallest mountain in the world 21 times. To me, this is unfathomable. A single ascent would seem rewarding enough. After his 20th ascent, Apa Sherpa was asked in an interview if the climb ever gets boring. He replied, "I am more familiar with the rocks and paths, yes, but no two journeys are ever the same." Perhaps scaling Everest 21 times by two able-bodied men doesn't impress you or incite you to become Professionally Driven. How about a quadruple amputee?

Kyle Maynard was born in 1986 with a condition known as congenital amputation. That is, he was born with no arms past his elbows and no legs past his knees. To have all four limbs not fully form before birth is very rare, but then again, everything about Kyle is unique.

Kyle's resume is impressive to say the least. He started an athletic career in youth football at nose guard. In sixth grade he joined the wrestling team, eventually tallying 36 wins his senior year and placing 12th at 103 pounds in the Georgia state wrestling tournament. He wrestled in college, and in 2004 was awarded the ESPY for Best Male Athlete with a Disability. In 2005, he wrote the New York Times Best Selling autobiography *No Excuses: The True Story of a Congenital Amputee Who Became a Champion in Wrestling and in Life*. From there, Kyle left college to pursue a career as a motivational speaker. He would later be a guest on the Oprah Winfrey Show and Larry King Live. To say that Kyle is **driven** is an understatement.

Despite all of his achievements, though, Kyle hit a plateau in his life, triggered by depression. In an ESPN special, Kyle described feeling like a phony to those he attempted to motivate when he, himself, could not feel the same. It wasn't until an encounter with two Iraq War veteran amputees on a plane that Kyle realized the positive effect he could have on others. "They told me that they were laying in a hospital bed for a week after they had been ambushed. They made a suicide pact with each other, and they said on the day they made that decision they happened to see my story, and that's what got them to stop." It was this encounter that made Kyle realize there was more to himself. Being driven means to perpetually see the glass half empty with the potential to be full. If we take the active steps to fill the glass, it will only spill over into others' cups, much like if they were stacked in the shape of a mountain.

In 2012, Kyle embarked on the very ambitious and laborious journey of scaling Mt. Kilimanjaro, the highest peak in Africa at 19,431 feet.

To come to a new understanding of himself, Kyle felt the need to climb a mountain. Kyle successfully climbed the mountain in ten days the only way he knew how, without the assistance of any prosthetics, just as he has lived his entire life. This accomplishment lead to his second ESPY for Best Male Athlete with a Disability in the same year of reaching the summit.

Dr. Cannon, Apa, Phurba, and Kyle are just four mountain climbing stories out of thousands. Stories of those who believed they could reach the summit and were motivated to take the first step. However, they needed to make sure the conditions to complete the trek were ideal. In a learning environment, we *can* create those ideal conditions for educators, conditions that empower educators to find that starting point and begin their journey.

REACHING MY SUMMIT

"I think we have everything hooked up right. You guys ready?" I say to the crew from Oelwein as the room begins to fill up.

"I think so. Let's go," a few of them reply.

The Keystone AEA, the area education agency that I work for, holds a conference every June as a service to the educators in our area of the state. Over the course of time, we have welcomed 700+ educators from the Midwest on a yearly basis. Originally, it started as a technology integration conference, but in 2016 we expanded it to encompass all areas of education and ultimately renamed it the Keystone Premier Education Conference (KPEC). In 2015, a mere six months after implementing the Professionally Driven model, I was presenting with Jill Kelly (Instructional Coach), Mary Beth Steggall (Middle School Principal @MrsSteggall), Lori Decker (Instructional Coach), Dianne Loughren (Teacher-Librarian @dmloughren), and Diane Sperfslage (Teacher-Librarian @dsperf). This group represented Oelwein with me as we presented to a room of about 60 educators what the Professionally Driven model was and how it was making an impact.

At one point in the presentation, we modeled for the participants the four phases by using the four walls to help differentiate the phases of the Professionally Driven model and had volunteers walk from one wall to the next as we explained what each phase means. We also displayed one of each of the flags that Oelwein uses to signify the recognition an educator receives at each phase.

The presentation was going very well until I was suddenly caught off guard. Participants were asking questions and trying to understand how all the pieces correlate in creating the journey. I was leading this part of the presentation, explaining the nuances between each phase. I gestured for one volunteer to move from the Reflection phase wall to join me up front, indicating she had completed her journey at the Sharing phase. Mary Beth held up the purple flag that educators at Oelwein receive when they complete their first journey. I thanked the volunteers and dismissed them back to their seats. Then Mary Beth spoke up. "So, Jarod. In putting together this model and helping us implement it, what did you have to do at each stage?" When she asked this, I was confused for two reasons:

1. I thought Jill was supposed to lead the next section of the presentation in order to discuss the coach's role in the model.
2. Mary Beth made it sound like she was confused as to what the four phases were, when in fact, she had completed her own full journey and has a purple flag of her own.

Confused, I continued to answer her question. "Well, we recognized that the current form of PD was not benefiting all educators in the district. So we thought of how we could improve it."

"Research phase, OK," she said, as if to review.

Assuming she wanted me to continue, I did. "We then implemented it with the staff while collecting survey responses periodically."

"Integration phase, OK. Did you share all of this inside our district?" she continued.

Was she asking me out loud to pretend that she was one of the audience members asking for clarification? I was still confused as to the purpose of going back through these four phases when we just got done explaining it to everyone.

But I answered anyway. "Yeah, we had to if we wanted everyone to be empowered with their learning."

She replied, "Reflection phase. And now that you have presented at this conference, you have shared outside our district, correct?" I nodded.

"You have completed your own journey, and therefore we would like to present you with your own purple flag." She smiled and handed me the purple flag that represented a full journey. It was even signed by our keynoter that day, Jennie Magiera (@MsMagiera).

I was stunned and gave her a hug as the educators in the room clapped. I'm not sure if the audience quite knew what the moment was all about, but I knew. The Oelwein team knew. And that was the moment when I realized that I had gone on my own Professionally Driven journey and hadn't even realized it. In order to develop this model and figure how it could truly empower every educator, I had naturally gone through all four phases. I thanked the Oelwein crew, and we finished the presentation.

Since that day, I have shared this model at multiple conferences, including ISTE in Denver. I have led multiple schools in our AEA area in implementing this model, as well other schools outside our area.

And while all of this would technically constitute as completing the Sharing phase, I have decided to take it another step farther.

While I am thankful that the Oelwein crew recognized my own journey and its completion, this book truly is the summit for me. It's the ultimate way for me to share what we have created and learned from empowering educators to truly be Professionally Driven. With this book, I hope we can create adult learning environments where the letters PD no longer stand for *Professional Development*: a static noun, a thing we do, something that is dreaded by most. But rather, it represents the educator: **Professionally Driven**. As one participant at my presentation at ISTE put it, Professionally Driven describes an active educator "who is always outgrowing their best teaching." I want *every* educator—both teachers and administrators—to own the letters and feel proud to say, "**I AM PD**."

CONTINUING THE JOURNEY

The Professionally Driven journey is never "complete." I wish to continue my journey by creating a hub for educators to share their journeys: another place for them to reach the Sharing phase. To this end, I have created a website for us to share our journeys: **professionallydriven.com**. Here you will be able to share your journey any way you wish. You want to write about your journey? We can post your writing. Willing to chat about your journey? We can do a video chat, record it, and post it. Created your own video? Perfect. Send it my way, and I will be sure to share it with our Professionally Driven community. By posting your journeys, you are sharing your new understanding/expertise to an audience of educators outside your district. Who knows, maybe you'll even help an educator identify their Point A.

At our website, you'll also find several handouts/posters that you can print for free in order to help plan for the Professionally Driven journey in your district. These handouts and posters are being used in numerous districts today. Our Professionally Driven community would love to see and hear your district's use and personalization of the model.

In Chapter 1, I mentioned my own hesitation in leaving the classroom in order to take an instructional technology position. I was worried that I wouldn't have that same sense of satisfaction that

I got from seeing those lightbulb moments with students or the relationships that I worked hard to establish. But when I work with a school to implement the Professionally Driven model, I get to see those same moments. I become energized and renewed when I hear of an educator that has completed a journey. I can't help but smile every time an educator excitedly tells me about their journey and how they have seen an improvement with learners. I get even more giddy when I hear an administrator has become a learner once again and has tackled an area that they felt could improve their building culture either on a micro or macro level.

My journey now has taken a new path up the same mountain. In 2016, a year after I presented this model at a state-wide educational technology conference in Iowa, I returned to the same conference to present on another subject. While I was downstairs helping run a booth for the University of Northern Iowa, a teacher stopped by and said she had attended my Professionally Driven session the year before. She also said that she took the model back to her district, and since then, they have implemented it and have seen great results with educators.

The focus of my journey now is to empower every educator and help share their successful journeys. It's these stories that intrinsically motivate me to continue to spread the model. In the Professionally Driven community, we encourage and embrace the sharing. I look forward to hearing your journey of success. The community benefits from hearing your journey, and by sharing your journey, others are encouraged to continue theirs. Connect with the Professionally Driven community and share your story at *professionallydriven.com* or connect on Twitter @jbormann3 and join us at #ProDriven to continue the discussion. Or if you want to implement the model but aren't sure how, get in touch, because we cannot give up on the original questions posed in Chapter 1:

What about us?
What about all learners?

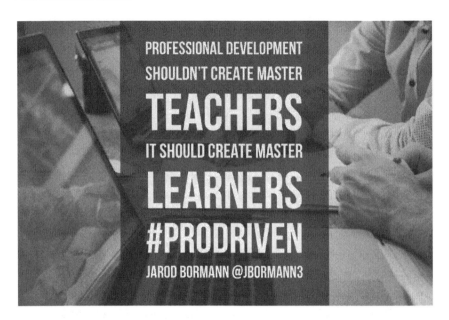

ABOUT THE AUTHOR

Jarod Bormann is a Technology Integration Specialist at the Keystone Area Education Agency in NE Iowa. He received his Masters in Instructional Technology through the University of Northern Iowa, and is currently an adjunct professor for the same masters program. Jarod taught middle school and high school English for seven years in one of the first 1:1 iPad schools in Iowa. He is an ISTE presenter and was recognized as the 2014 Iowa Safe Schools Educator of the Year. Jarod blogs at bormannbytes.com and professionallydriven.com. An annual presenter at the Keystone KPEC Conference, Iowa Technology & Education Connection (ITEC Featured Speaker), as well as other educational tech conferences throughout the midwest, he is an ITEC Iowa Board Member and co-hosts the *Next Level Learning* podcast. Connect with Jarod via Twitter **@jbormann3** or email **jarod@professionallydriven.com**

More from
The Bretzmann Group

Personalized PD: Flipping Your Professional Development

What should professional development look like? Can all teachers get exactly what they need? How do we energize every individual to realize their full potential?

Personalized PD: Flipping Your Professional Development helps answer these questions and more. Seven authors start from the premise that teachers are learners who learn at different paces and start in different places. Personalized PD helps each individual teacher move toward self-determined goals.

The authors take you through their experiences while giving you their best "pro tips" and most useful technology tools. They'll save you time and research by pointing you in the right direction right now. Each chapter gives you a window into how these practicing educators execute their plan to get every teacher what they need and move each individual toward their own plan of learning. Plus, short vignettes expand on and go deeper into the most useful tools and techniques.

Come join the conversation, and be part of the fundamental change in professional development we call CHOICE (Constant progress, Honoring professionals, Ongoing learning, Individualized focus, Collaborative learning, Energizing experiences).

Personalized PD: Flipping Your Professional Development will help you get there.

Find this book at **bit.ly/personalizedPD**

Personalized PD: Game of Stories

The game that is taking over every professional development experience to make it more fun, energizing, and collaborative.

Build capacity while building community with this unique and entertaining game. Hear the stories of your colleagues while reflecting on your own development as an educator. Get the conversation started about how to move your building and your district forward. Honor the professionals you work with every day by listening to their progress and their process as educators.

Everybody has something to contribute. Everybody has something to learn. You might win the game, but you might win more by losing!

Play *Personalized PD: Game of Stories* today and take your professional development to a whole new level.

Find this game at **tinyurl.com/ppdstories**   #GoStories

Flipping 2.0: Practical Strategies for Flipping Your Class

With a foreword by Aaron Sams. If you've decided to flip your class, you probably have new questions: How do I do this? What will it look like? What will students do in class? How will I create learning experiences for students outside of class? What have other teachers done?

Flipping 2.0: Practical Strategies for Flipping Your Class seeks to answer your questions. And it opens the dialogue for us to continue to learn together.

In this book, you will follow practicing classroom teachers as they walk you through their flipped classroom journey; why and how they made the change, what obstacles they overcame, the technology they used, and where they are heading next. As a flipped learning teacher, you need time to check out workable solutions that other teachers have created.

Look inside their classrooms and learn from their experiences. Watch flipped teachers at work. Pick the brains of those who've been there, and join the conversation. You'll find something useful in every chapter.

And there is a chapter just for you in this book, including English, math, science, social studies, world languages, technology, Google tools, mastery learning, elementary, middle school, part-time flipping, and even professional development.

Read *Flipping 2.0* today and make your decision to flip a reality.

Find this book at **bit.ly/flipping20** and **tinyurl.com/flipping20**

*Please contact **jbretzmann@bretzmanngroup.com** for more information or for special discounts on any Bretzmann Group item when purchased in quantity.*

WWW.BRETZMANNGROUP.COM

29563500R00094

Made in the USA
Lexington, KY
31 January 2019